EATING
FAMOUSLY

To Janet

18.2.2011

Memories

Best Wishes

Elena

EATING FAMOUSLY

Elena Salvoni
on fabulous food for her famous friends and
diners…and a lifetime in Soho restaurants

by Chris Wright • Mike Maloney • William Hall

EATING FAMOUSLY

First published in 2007 by Walnut West One Limited in London, England

© **Walnut West One Limited**

Some elements of this book were researched from the book 'Elena – A Life in Soho', by Sandy Fawkes, published by Quartet Books in 1986

The editorial content of Eating Famously is exclusively sourced from the best recollections and archives of Elena Salvoni and in no way seeks to infer or suggest endorsement of any kind by any individual or organisation.

Written by: **William Hall**
Original and food photography: **Mike Maloney OBE**
Creative concept, editorial, art and production direction: **Chris Wright**
Special contribution: **Neil Fennell**

Design: **Paul Cooper Design**
All celebrity archive images: **Rex Features**

 www.rexfeatures.com

For sales and all other enquiries please visit
www.eatingfamously.co.uk

Contents

Contents

Foreword

When I first met Elena she was already a legend in her own lunchtime, and indeed many other people's lunchtimes as well. Her presence as maitresse d' had turned the cramped and unpretentious dining room at Bianchi's in Frith Street into the venue of choice for the leading lights of theatre, literature and television.

It was not until she moved to L'Escargot that I got to know Elena and began to understand what it was about her that made her the centre of a galaxy of bright, talented, complex, competitive people, turned the walls of the restaurant into a mini-National Portrait Gallery and the reservations book into a Who's Who of the West End.

First and foremost, Elena is superb at her job. In an age when so many eye-catching, expensive establishments seem to believe that chic design and robotic black-clad waiters are enough, she personifies the simple fact that a good maitre d' is essential, indeed indispensable for a good restaurant.

Elena's skills are in play long before the punters arrive. She is a virtuoso in the fine art of table placing. Knowing most of her clientele well (because, like me, they keep coming back) her ear is carefully attuned to nuances of changing circumstances and relationships. She knows exactly when playwrights and producers have fallen out or which actors have been chosen for the plum roles and which haven't, and by whom. I'm sure there are times when she misjudges her positioning, but I'm equally sure that there have been productions, performances, books and articles that would not have happened without Elena's sixth sense of where best to seat her guests.

Once you arrive at the restaurant, her welcome can brighten the most miserable day. It is always perfectly judged, as if she knows your mood even before you cross the threshold. And it is a personal welcome, so different from the glassy, quickly-dying smiles that too often pass for a greeting these days.

I'm trying to resist the "m" word, but yes, she was bit of a mother figure to us all in the early days. She did regard those she saw frequently as "my boys" and "my girls", I'm sure and she took an interest in our careers which was natural and sincere and never calculated or contrived. She was straightforward and never sycophantic. I felt that I could share thoughts and feelings with Elena and get the truth from her. And I'm sure I wasn't the only one.

Elena loves the creative world of theatre, films and television, but she is at home with anybody. We celebrated my mother's 80th birthday at L'Escargot. Elena and my mother got on immediately – they were both small and made each other laugh a lot – and thanks to her a whole crowd of friends, relatives, out-of-town cousins and others who didn't know each other were instantly put at ease.

Elena, entirely in character, wrote and asked me if I wouldn't mind writing 'just a few words" by way of introduction to this book, and, I'm afraid, I've failed. It's impossible to sum up this remarkable lady in just a few words. Honesty, hard work, high standards and a natural, unselfconscious pleasure in people and the lives they lead are the qualities that have put her at the top of her profession and made her so many friends. They're not dramatic or extraordinary qualities but in this rushed and pressured world they are increasingly rare. Which makes Elena a national treasure. Well, certainly a metropolitan treasure.

Can I have the best table now, please?

Michael Palin

Denville Hall
Home for Retired Actors

Denville Hall at Northwood in Middlesex, is a charity founded and run by actors for their profession. It has been funded through the kindness of actors and theatre managers since 1925.

Since 1965, The Actors' Charitable Trust, TACT has assisted in the running of the Hall. TACT is a charity that helps actors' children, and in that role it had extensive experience of running orphanages. Although separate charities, TACT and Denville Hall are closely linked in that they share Trustees.

Lord Attenborough, who is a Trustee and Sir John Mills, a great supporter who lived nearby in Denham Village, introduced Elena to Denville Hall when the first floor private room at Elena's L'Etoile was dedicated to British Oscar Winners in 1996. Since then, everyone using the room makes a contribution to Denville Hall and Elena makes regular visits to see both the staff and residents.

Denville Hall prides itself on its special atmosphere. It places the greatest value on the dignity and happiness of its residents: the Hall is their home and residents are given the greatest say possible in how their daily lives at Denville should be.

Bought by Alfred Denville, impresario, actor-manager and MP. He dedicated the Hall to the acting profession, in memory of his son Jack, who had died at the age of 26 after an injury on stage reactived earlier damage sustained in the Great War. The hall was renamed Denville Hall, and opened fully in 1926. Denville Hall became a charity in 1925.

Eligibility for admission is based on theatrical history and medical criteria. For more detailed information see the Denville Hall website: www.denvillehall.org
email: denvillehall@yahoo.com or call the Home Administrator, Mrs Julie Bignell on 01923 825 843.

Part of the profits of 'Eating Famously' will go to Denville Hall.

My Tribute

Kevin Hopgood

*E*ating *Famously* is my tribute to all the customers and colleagues who have given me such a wonderful life in Soho's restaurants. I hope some of my better known customers, many of whom have become lifelong friends, will be happy and perhaps a little amused by just a few of the countless memories of occasions and incidents that have come to mind in looking back over my many years in the business.

Which brings me to the reason we all come together – the wonderful food. So this is also my tribute to the culinary skills of all the chefs and their teams wherever I have worked. Here I've chosen just some of my favourite dishes from the repertoire of Kevin Hopgood, Thomas Musiiwa and Sami Bourai, all of whom have worked with me here at Elena's L'Etoile.

Over the years I've found that being a good maitre'd usually involves three things. First and foremost, everyone must have a really good welcome.

If possible – and they are not deep in conversation – I also like to stop for a chat with as many people as possible sometime during their visit – usually between courses if I can. Third, I try to take as many orders as I can – and even now I carefully write them down. It's amazing how often people say they go to a restaurant and don't get what they ordered. It also helps me to remember the dishes different customers like best.

Thomas Musiiwa & Sami Bourai

It's also amazing how many people look at the menu and then ask me to suggest something they'd like. So often, people like food which matches their personality and I usually recommend dishes that way. For regulars, it's easy because I know their favourites. But for people I meet for the first time I take a cue from how they look and how they sound – happy – sad – relaxed – even stressed! You can tell a lot from a person's demeanour just by looking and listening.

So for the recipes in my book I thought it would be a novel idea to suggest a dish for each of my well known friends and diners that we've featured in the book. Of course, some have particular favourites as you'll see. I hope they all like my choice… and some of the photographs I've found of their many memorable performances.

Complementing the food is the service… and again I pay tribute to all my talented front of house staff, especially Andreas, Costa, Manuel, Geraldo, Peggy and all the team who work tirelessly to ensure that everyone enjoys their time in our restaurant.

This moment couldn't pass without me thanking Aldo, Adriana, Luis and all my family and many friends for playing such a big part in my life in restaurants.

To my dear friend Michael Palin, thank you for such kind thoughts and words. To Neil Fennell, thank you for your confidence and generous support in helping bring this book to reality.

I would also especially like to thank William Hall for helping me to recall so many memorable experiences and put them into words; Mike Maloney for bringing all our dishes to mouthwatering life in his stunning photographs; and Chris Wright for creating such an interesting and unusual way to tell my story and making it happen.

Long may we all continue *Eating Famously*.

Elena Salvoni

Biography – A Life in Soho Restaurants

" Darling Elena, Purveyor of Scrumptiousness to
the Discerning (and an old girlfriend)
...by Appointment to Dame Edna Everage "

BARRY HUMPHRIES

Elena Salvoni has been dubbed the "Queen of Soho" by newspapers and her star-studded clients alike, and with good reason. The woman who has run celebrity restaurants for more than 50 years of her eventful life once said: "Most of the people who are lucky enough to discover Soho fall in love with the place."

She proceeded to do so, and stayed for half a century to consummate her love affair with London's famous – or notorious – square mile.

Elena was born on April 29 1920 in Clerkenwell, a bustling cosmopolitan area of East London within a stone's throw of the City where, in those days, the only phone in the entire area belonged to a grocer – who also doubled his income as a bookie.

The family became part of the Italian community. Her father Luigo Maestri was a builder with a head for heights, specialising in laying asphalt on rooftops, while her mother Rosina ran a boarding house. Elena met her future husband Aldo at school – his own father sold blocks of ice from a horse and cart in the nearby streets. Elena's own terraced home had an outside toilet, while the washing was done in a huge copper vat in the scullery, to be hung outside in the yard to dry.

"There were no such things as mod cons in those days," Elena recalls. "But I had a marvellous childhood. Mama made wonderful risottos, other families in the streets made great pizzas, and we all ate in each other's houses. Nobody would have starved while there was still enough flour in the larder to make pasta."

She went to St Peter's Italian School, one of 1200 pupils made up of Italian, Greek, Irish and English, and now known as Catherine's School of Dance. Above all, the streets were safe. "Nobody would have molested a child".

Because there was little traffic the children would stretch heavy brewer's ropes across the road to use as a giant skipping rope, while soccer-mad boys would use bundles of newspaper tied up with string as primitive footballs. Today Elena talks nostalgically

> " Most of the people who are lucky enough to discover Soho fall in love with the place. "

Elena (3rd from right, second row) at St Peter's Italian School School, 1927.

With the family at Nick Lander's L'Escargot party for Elena. From left: son in law Brian, daughter in law Jeanette, Elena, husband Aldo, son Luis and daughter Adriana.

about skipping-rope rhymes like *Silk, Satin, Cotton, Rags* – "whichever one you tripped up on was what you were going to be married in!"

The Church was the centre of their lives, and Elena still meets up every year at the Italian procession for the Feast of Our Lady of Mount Carmel. "In those days the procession could be a mile long. Now I still go to a service every Sunday". But the heart of her life was the family, and the most important weekly ritual was Sunday lunch – "we had wine with the meals, but mine was watered because I was little!"

Food and wine from an early age obviously played a vital part in young Elena's upbringing, even if she wasn't aware of it. Maybe it laid the ground stone for her eventual foray into the heady world of wining and dining, where she would become the most famous restaurant hostess in the whole of London, meeting and greeting the famous and the infamous with the warm smile of welcome that made her an intrinsic part of the social scene.

Eventually, anyone who was anyone would know Elena, and she would know them. But first, back in those wartime days, there was a marriage to attend – her own, to her childhood friend Aldo – and the start of another career that fizzled out almost before it began.

Elena left school in the summer of 1934, aged fourteen, and started her first job a week later. There was work aplenty – the Italian community looked after its own, and fathers found jobs for their sons among their own friends, and mothers did likewise for their daughters.

Before she knew it, the young Elena found herself as a Mayfair seamstress working for a Mr Arnaldi of Dorville Models, learning the intricacies of pin-tucking and hem stitching. And all for seven shillings and sixpence a week, of which she gave her Mama five shillings. "We all wore white arm-cuffs so as not to mark the material," is a vivid memory that has stayed with her for seven decades. "I went to work on the No 73 bus, and the fare was twopence!"

Elena's future husband was more interested in sport. He had been a stalwart in the school soccer team, with a number of trophies in the library to show for it. He even won a Jack Hobbs bat for his cricketing prowess, no

Elena and Aldo cut their wedding cake at Reggories, Kings Cross on 20th April 1941.

mean feat, along with a certificate the couple still have framed in their Islington home.

But it was dancing that brought them together – literally. Elena was part of a "girl gang" who went dancing every weekend with boys as escorts, and she finally persuaded the reluctant Aldo to join the group. He took to it like a fish to water – "and when he was confident enough he asked me to partner him. We got on famously. I wouldn't want to say we were childhood sweethearts, but we had played together in the streets, our mothers were great friends, and we just spent more and more time together."

And she adds fondly: "Secretly I thought that he looked just like Clark Gable in his dashing white silk evening scarf!" Eventually the couple would become expert ballroom dancers, and win awards at contests throughout the UK – so maybe some of the judges thought the same.

They were married at St Peter's on April 20 1941, in the height of the Blitz – ironically, as Elena found out later, on Hitler's birthday. "But the Führer decided not to be sentimental about his birthday or my wedding day, and the bombing began at nine am."

It continued as the wedding party were forced to evacuate the reception

> **"But the Führer decided not to be sentimental about his birthday or my wedding day, and the bombing began at nine am."**

13

at a restaurant in King's Cross and troop up Pentonville Road to carry on the festivities at home "with me still in my wedding dress". The redoubtable couple would move into a small flat in the area, and see the war out, despite several narrow escapes. "One particularly nasty bomb was called a Molotov Basket, which sent small firebombs scattering in all directions when it landed. One hit our back bedroom, and we were just lucky the whole place didn't go up.

> ## " I received no wages, and was expected to survive on tips. "

"That night the bombs were coming down at the rate of one a minute, and we all ran for shelter in the Angel tube station. In the morning when we emerged into daylight, I'll never forget the sight of all the trees covered in white ash and festooned with people's belongings. But somehow we survived the Blitz."

Their daughter Adriana was born in 1943, and it was a year later that Elena was to find her true calling: in the Café Bleu in Old Compton Street in the heart of Soho, with Mama back home minding the baby. The job was on the bottom rung of the ladder, as a waitress, but she somehow felt at home, even in her element.

She made the uniforms for herself and five other waitresses – royal blue pinafore dresses over crisp; white blouses. "I received no wages, and was expected to survive on tips. And how I found the time to dash home each afternoon and put the baby to bed, I'll never know!"

The uniforms matched the décor – the Café Bleu had royal blue tiles, shell-shaped wall lights made of glass, and sparkling white cloths on the sixteen tables. With covers for 60 customers, it was a busy place with a regular complement of British and French servicemen and American GIs looking for relaxation and pasta.

The Café Bleu became a haunt for artists, writers, actors and Bohemians, including star names like actors Michael Redgrave and Terence de Marney and "characters" like Jeffrey Bernard who became regulars.

Café Bleu.

café bleu
40 old compton street :: london :: w.1.

The Café Bleu 1945 Christmas Card on which Quentin Joyce- brother of William "Lord Haw-Haw" Joyce wrote: To Elena, the Mighty Atom.

One individual Elena remembers with mixed feelings was a customer named Quentin Joyce, whom she later discovered was the brother of William ("Lord Haw-Haw") Joyce, the infamous broadcaster of Hitler's wartime propaganda with his notorious call-sign "Germany calling! Germany calling!" nightly on the airwaves.

"After the war ended Quentin came in one day late looking very agitated, and demanded lunch at once. He had just come from a vigil outside the prison where Lord Haw-Haw had been hanged that morning! It was very bizarre and quite chilling. That Christmas he left me a card which said: *To Elena, the Mighty Atom.* I never knew why, but I kept the card and still have it to this day."

In the food shortage following the war the black market flourished in the vibrant atmosphere of the "Little Italy" community, just as it did throughout Soho and Elena often lived on her wits.

She recalls how she made her family "delicious and nourishing meals of spaghetti, meatballs and stew. After all, they were very rich in protein!" She also saw her share of the dark underbelly of Soho life. One notorious character she regularly served was bookmaker Albert Dimes, who ten years later would become a legend after a ferocious knife-fight in the street with a rival named Jack "Spot" Comer, which left the pavement literally awash with blood and onlookers sluicing the road with buckets of water. The fight had been over control of Soho's sleazy night clubs, and ended with both men in

Elena at her mother's original Singer sewing machine (circa 1911) which still sees regular service. Elena made all the net curtains for L'Etoile...in her 'spare' time.

hospital and "Spottie" having 280 stitches. "Perhaps this is why Albert was a regular at Café Bleu, but I never actually laid eyes on Comer. You could say that the two never did get on!"

Two years after she began there, the Café Bleu burned down. Elena knew nothing of it until she arrived for work as usual, to find the building a smouldering hulk. It seemed the fire had been sparked off by an electrical fault under the stairs. "It was a terrible shock. And somehow it didn't seem fair when I thought of how the restaurant had survived the war and the worst of the Blitz. But I had to get on with my own life – and that meant returning to the sewing machine."

Another, far worse, blow was when her beloved Mama died soon after. Elena inherited her mother's old Singer treadle-worked sewing machine that Luigi had given his wife for their first wedding anniversary back in 1911. "In a curious way sitting in the front room working it was comforting to me. I still have it – and still use it! Aldo has often offered to buy me an electric machine, but I'm happy and content with the old one, and for me it's my connection with the past."

Today Elena keeps the Singer in an upstairs room in their Islington house, with one of Mama's pillow overlays draped over it to keep the dust out. "It's not a pillow-case," she'll tell you firmly. "But the beautifully hand-embroidered lace-edged cloth she would use to cover each pillow during the daytime. We may have lived in virtual hovels – but oh, how proud Italian women were of their linen and lace!"

Apart from the Singer and its practical use, Elena has other memories of the old days: "Boxes and boxes of newspaper cuttings about the customers who became my friends, and albums full of pictures of them. I'm the most terrible hoarder – I can't bear to throw away a single postcard or letter. The way I see it, when people bother to think of you from the other side of the world, their kindness is worth treasuring."

> **❝ Even today, though I no longer wait at tables, the job of welcoming customers, taking their orders and discussing the menu still gives me immense pleasure. ❞**

Three years later, Elena abandoned her sewing machine and went back into the business she loved – and where she would stay for the next half-century and more. This was 1951. A phone call to an old friend brought the news that Bianchi's famous restaurant in the heart of Soho was in a panic:

three waitresses had somehow all gone off on holiday at the same time, and the place was desperately short-staffed. The manager of Café Bleu, Mr Paccini, had joined Bianchi's, and Elena was taken on immediately with no questions asked or references required. "I rang him on Friday, and started on the Monday!"

She was in her element, and soon rose from waitress to helping Mr Paccini greet the customers. "Even today, though I no longer wait at tables, the job of welcoming customers, taking their orders and discussing the menu still gives me immense pleasure," she says.

The clientele was familiar. Mr Bianchi had opened his restaurant in 1928, serving simple Italian dishes in ground floor premises looking out through picture windows on to bustling Frith Street. By the time Elena joined he had expanded on to the first floor, and the menu had expanded too. "It was a happy restaurant," Elena recalls with more than a hint of nostalgia. "Both the rooms were light and airy, with those big windows and large mirrors. It was hugely popular with theatrical people as well as artists and writers." This explained the posters and signed photographs that hung on the walls – an

Bianchi's, Frith Street.

impressive feature that Elena employs at her L'Etoile restaurant today.

"It was here that I began numerous lifelong friendships, many of them extending over three generations," she says, remembering the celebrities who trooped past the reception desk to be escorted to their tables. The list reads like a roll-call for "Night of a Hundred Stars": Michael Wilding, Margaret Leighton, Dame Sybil Thorndike and her husband Lewis Casson, Lilli Palmer, Maria Callas, Sean Connery, Tony Dalli, all the way through to Bud Abbott and Lou Costello…and that, as they say in the restaurant business, was just for starters.

Bud and Lou decided to make Bianchi's the place to celebrate their opening night when they appeared for a week at the London Palladium, one of a series of major Hollywood stars who trod the Palladium boards in those heady days, among them Danny Kaye and Laurel and Hardy. Elena happened to be looking out of the open upstairs window when she saw their car arrive.

Bianchi's Italian Café enjoys its new era as Bar Italia.

Ella Fitzgerald at Bianchi's with Elena, Aldo and members of her band during a season at Ronnie Scott's during the 70's.

Little Lou looked up, caught her eye and said loudly: "Here, d'ere's a boid lookin' at us!" Inside they kept up the banter, noisily referring to Elena as "our boid!" throughout the rest of the evening.

A less salubrious star was Donald Maclean, the other half of the Burgess and Maclean spy scandal that rocked the country in 1951. "Maclean and his wife Melinda had lunch at Bianchi's just two days before his defection story broke. Two days! All I can say is that they appeared totally relaxed and at ease, without a hint of tension or anxiety about them. They sat at table 5 under the clock. I was amazed when I read the sordid details. Looking at him, you would never have suspected."

Scandal of a different nature involved a couple Elena noticed who came in for dinner one night. "Maybe it's just instinct, but I have a sixth sense when something is – well, not quite right," she says. "It hovers over people like an aura, invisible and inexplicable. This young couple looked supremely happy, as if they were celebrating – but not in a noisy way. In the early editions of the evening papers next day I saw their faces plastered over Page 1 – James Goldsmith and Isobel Patino had eloped! Nice that they chose Bianchi's for a consummation of their romance, I remember thinking…"

Elena remembers how tables 12 and 15 were favourites with politicians and political journalists. "They were tucked into the corners of the big downstairs room, ideal for discreet conversations." Since many on the periphery of government were anonymous faces, she had no idea who they were and occasionally suffered the consequences.

"People mostly paid by cash as there were no credit cards in those days, not even cheque cards. One day a gentleman named Derek Mitchell presented a cheque. I asked him to put his address on the back as was the usual practice, but when I got to the cash desk and looked at it I saw he'd written: '10, Downing Street'.

"I marched straight back to his table and demanded: "'What's all this?'

"He smiled and replied: 'I'm Harold Wilson's press secretary, Elena. Didn't you know?'" Well no, I didn't. Laughter all round.

"But I got my revenge by telling him he had better watch his step - because he was sitting in the hot seat occupied by Mandy Rice-Davies the previous day while the Old Bailey trial involving Christine Keeler was going on."

With Mrs John Logie Baird.

Another claim to fame for Bianchi's was its role in John Logie Baird's discovery of television. Elena is seen here with his wife. The very first TV picture was transmitted by the great man between two rooms in one of the flats above Bianchi's!! This 'blue plaque' can be seen there today, where Bianchi's 'Italian Café' has long since become the well known 'Bar Italia,' famous with a whole new generation of Soho devotees.

After a couple of years at Bianchi's Elena was promoted to assistant manager, which meant no more waitressing and a lot of meeting and greeting. "This gave me the chance to help the young kids struggling to survive at the start of their careers. Or, even more frequently when it came to actors and artists, going through a bad patch financially or emotionally.

"Many was the time I loaded tables with extra rolls and butter for young actors and dancers coming in late after the show, hungry and hard up. Anyone can fall on hard times, and I've watched fortunes disappear like water down a drain. But most of these youthful and talented people went on to do well – and, of course, remain my regular customers."

The cast list unrolls… Paul Scofield ("a natural gentleman – and *so* patient"), French heart-throb Louis Jourdan ("the waitresses went all a-flutter"), the legendary Charles Laughton ("he frightened the life out of everyone with his overwhelming presence"), Simone Signoret, apparently recommended to the restaurant by Laurence Harvey ("a very womanly woman, but I could never

"Maybe it's just instinct, but I have a sixth sense when something is – well, not quite right."

understand why she became so overweight"), David McCallum ("I had no idea he was the star of *The Man from UNCLE*. To me he was just that nice-looking boy who used to come in with his parents!")…

Heart-throbs galore, male and female, walked off the screen and into Bianchi's in those pulsating days of the fifties and sixties, turning heads, creating murmurs of recognition, most of them milking the adulation that went with it.

Many have stayed the course to remain Elena's friend for five decades. Albert Finney, for one. She recalls the regular in-joke they swap, from the actor whose first love is still the horses, when he'll give her that wicked smile straight out of *Tom Jones* and remark: "Elena, do you remember when we were poor?"

> " Heart-throbs galore, male and female, walked off the screen and into Bianchi's in those pulsating days of the fifties and sixties. "

Of course she does. Instead she gives him a nudge and a laugh, and replies: "A bookmaker's son is never poor!"

Elena witnessed for herself the subtle change in Soho that began in the sixties with the appearance of the Establishment Club in Greek Street. Soho had always been a demanding mistress, a scarlet lady who was both duchess and tart, and you had to know her to survive. A shamelessly decadent square mile, she was a village by day, bustling with activity complete with its own bakery, dairy, fruit-and-vegetable market, laundry and newsagent's – and someone else by night. Razor gangs were a frightening part of the scene – the "violent subculture" as it was called - though they normally only used to deal with their own in dark corners and back alleys in a confrontation over territory or a woman.

Elena vividly remembers the days - and nights - after the war when this square mile had been notorious as a red light district. A jumble of narrow streets with open doorways giving passers-by a glimpse of creaking stairs and threadbare carpets – and all kinds of temptation inside.

Along with ambiguous notices like "Big Chest for Sale" or "Rare Butterfly needs Mounting", there would be the inevitable dyed-hair blonde teetering on four-inch stilettos leaning casually against the railings with a murmured invitation to investigate the premises within.

With the arrival of the Establishment Club, all this changed – if not overnight, then irrevocably for the future. The face of Soho had a new, sophisticated air about it. Other clubs would spring up to follow in its footsteps. Candle-lit coffee bars sprouted like hothouse plants, and Espresso was the buzz-word with Lonnie Donegan becoming the acknowledged king of skiffle at the Two I's in Old Compton Street, where Tommy Steele was discovered.

As Elena remembers it: "The kind of people who normally wouldn't be seen dead outside Mayfair started to discover us, and the new vitality was reflected in people's clothes and manners. Suddenly Soho was 'the' place to be. The restaurants and clubs were like a catwalk, and the streets were full of socialites and the Chelsea set parading in the latest fashions."

The influence of the Establishment Club crowd brought not only a touch of class, but a new clientele to the area. "They were fun people, and many would become lifelong friends," she recalls. Among them were Johnny Dankworth and Cleo Laine. One lunchtime the pair started an improvised jam session with spoons and forks, glasses and coffee cups. Mr Bianchi wanted to stop them – but I told him to leave them alone. 'They're only young and having fun,' I said. And he let them carry on, while other tables joined in."

With names like Ned Sherrin, Alan Bennett, David Frost, David Hockney, Daniel Farson, George Melly and Francis Bacon making the party lively, the Soho scene thrived anew. Another long time follower of Elena since the Bianchi days is well known TV agent Jon Roseman. He's even named one of his children 'Ellie' after Elena and often uses L'Etoile like a second office, knowing his celebrity clients will feel just as much at home as he does.

One day at Bianchi's, a journalist said to Elena, "that's John Le Carré sitting over there isn't it?" "No," said Elena, "that's David Cornwall. He comes in quite often." Indeed it was John Le Carré but he always booked under his real name and still does!

For Elena, with love, admiration and long, long memories, all good – David – aka. John Le Carré

Deep I thought David Cornwall... better known as John Le Carré.

> ❝The kind of people who normally wouldn't be seen dead outside Mayfair started to discover us, and the new vitality was reflected in people's clothes and manners.❞

Elena at a party in 1986 with Lord and Lady Wilson and The Hon Charles Morris. Mary Wilson was a great friend.

Alan Bennett and David Hockney at Bianchi's in the 70's.

Back home in Clerkenwell, Elena and Aldo found further celebrity on their doorstep: the house next door had been rebuilt into four flats, and two new neighbours moved in: Joe Orton and Kenneth Halliwell. "They would come to tea on Sundays and show us newspaper cuttings of Joe's plays," Elena recalls. "They were an enchanting couple of boys. You can imagine my shock when I came home for my afternoon break one day to find police and TV cameras everywhere – Ken had killed Joe with a hammer, then taken his own life with an overdose! It was terrible. It had all happened in the room next to our bedroom the night before, and we never heard a thing."

In the fifties Bianchi's became a home from home for the boxing fraternity. The heavyweight, legendary Rocky Marciano led the field, with Henry Cooper and world champions like Carmen Basillio, Willie Pastrano, Jack "Kid" Berg and Joey Giardello in close attendance. They all liked their pasta, as well as the atmosphere. And they all signed a pair of boxing gloves that Elena has kept for that purpose.

"Trying to tell a drunk that he's had enough is one of the most difficult tasks in the world." With this sage statement Elena recalls wild times at Bianchi's – and later at L'Escargot and L'Etoile, after fifty years of proving it for herself. But with the skill of a diplomat and the firmness of a mother hen, she usually managed to keep the inebriates under control. But not always.

"Sometimes people get abusive in drink, and sometimes just plain silly," she says. Glamorous TV personality Selena Scott was there the night one guest threw a melon at the head of a fellow diner on the same first-floor table. "Naturally the man ducked, and there was a shattering of glass as the thing went through the window! I told them all to behave themselves, then ran down the stairs to see if anyone had been hurt. A melon is heavy, and if it

In the fifties Bianchi's became a home from home for the boxing fraternity.

had hit a passer-by on the head it could have knocked them out. Luckily there was no-one lying flat out on the pavement…"

Elena was in the front line to witness another fire: in the food lift shaft. "It happened one lunch time. The bell rang to inform me that the food was on the way up. I opened the dumb-waiter, and was appalled when smoke came belching out. From then on it was a madhouse! The fire had started half way up the lift, and I was chucking buckets of water down it while the chef, unaware of what was happening, was hollering up thinking I had gone barmy! Every time he tried to put plates on the shelf he got drenched. Finally I put the fire out by myself before the fire brigade arrived, with the waiters racing up three flights of stairs to serve the food! The firemen told me I was lucky to be alive as the water could have conducted the electric current back to me. Fortunately I always wear rubber soles, which saved me. But I was pretty shaken after that little episode."

A bigger fire months later closed Bianchi's for three weeks after a pan of fat burst into flames in the kitchen. "The customers grabbed all their bottles off the tables before fighting their way through the smoke and out into the street!"

L'Escargot, Greek Street.

There was another face to Soho: the Italian-Catholic connection, which had always been a strong bond. Father Bill Kirkpatrick started a refuge for the young homeless in St Anne's Crypt which he called Centrepoint, and Elena made a point of packing any rolls and bread left over from the night into a bag and dropping the bundle off on her way to catch the last bus home.

L'Escargot restaurant re-opened in 1981, and went on to become one of Soho's most famous restaurants. Elena joined owner Nick Lander as meeter and greeter, and opened another chapter in her career, seeing all her old friends and making many new ones.

Less familiar faces, though hugely distinguished in their own fields, were a set who formed themselves into the "Cranium Club" – a unique

> " L'Escargot restaurant re-opened in 1981, and went on to become one of Soho's most famous restaurants. "

Elena and Nick Lander at L'Escargot.

Ella Fitzgerald meets 'her' idol Gene Wilder at L'Escargot in 1985.

fellowship of professors and experts who met every three months at L'Escargot for earnest discussions on world events. They included such luminaries as Professor Freddie Ayer, Sir Lawrence Gowing, Sir Isaiah Berlin, Solly Zuckerman, Sir William Coldstream and Stephen Spender – who would become another regular at L'Etoile when Elena moved there.

The bad apple in this impressive academic basket was one Sir Anthony Blunt, later unfrocked as the notorious "fourth man" in the spy ring scandal that shook the Establishment in the seventies. "The revelation must have been as much of a shock to them as it was to me," Elena recalls.

Household names filled L'Escargot, from international celebrities to Britain's own TV fireside favourites: Ella Fitzgerald, Gene Wilder, Alan Jay Lerner, Melvyn (now Lord) Bragg, Peter O'Toole, Moira Fraser, Bernard Levin, Janet Suzman, Derek Jacobi, Barbara Windsor, Christopher Lee, Ian (now Sir Ian) McKellen, Maurice Denham, Michael and Mary Parkinson…the list was endless.

In the eighties the Queen of Soho met the Queen of England, at a garden party at Buckingham Palace. "All I could think of was: for heaven's sake, Elena, curtsey! And somehow I managed it." Elena was made an MBE in the 2006 New Year's Honours and returned to the palace to receive her award

Elena with Aldo at the cash desk by L'Escargot's famous "stairs". It was here that Peter Ustinov penned this self portrait for Aldo...with friendship.

Elena is introduced to HM The Queen by good friend, Sir William Heseltine at a garden party to celebrate the 400th anniversary of the City of Westminster. Soho restaurants joined together to provide the buffet.

from HRH The Prince of Wales 'for services to the hospitality industry.' This time Aldo and the family were at her side.

Ask Elena how she keeps the energy and enthusiasm to stay in her "second home" in London's colourful square mile, and she replies simply: "My blood is bonded to Soho – where at least no-one is ever going to die of boredom!" That for sure.

When it comes to fashion, Elena has noted the sea change in her customers' apparel. "All those young men earning a small fortune in the advertising world who come in - but you'd never suspect it from their turn-out – bomber jackets, jeans and trainers. It doesn't worry me. It's their uniform, and if they feel comfortable that's fine by me. Clothes don't make the person, manners do."

She also can't help noticing the changing face of the streets she knows like the back of her hand: "Silly T-shirt stores where there used to be family shops. But the heart of Soho is its people - the devotees!"

In 1994 Elena made her third and, she swears, her final move to yet another establishment which would profit by her arrival — and prove it by giving her name to

it. Elena's L'Etoile at No 30, Charlotte Street, is a stone's throw from Soho in Fitzrovia, an equally historic and cosmopolitan haunt of the media and showbusiness circle and paradise for those aficionados wishing to give vent to their taste buds. Italian rubs shoulders with French, Greek, Korean and Japanese.

She gave up L'Escargot, and in a single night took her collection of famous photographs down from the walls with the staff, her family and friends helping her to move them in boxes in two vans at 1.00am. They remained stored in a basement at her Islington home until she could put them back in the public gaze at L'Etoile eighteen months later.

The Gay Hussar in Greek Street.

GREEK STREET W1
CITY OF WESTMINSTER

"I went to work at the Gay Hussar in Greek Street. The owner and entrepreneur Roy Ackerman was eager to find me a place of my own. 'Come on, Elena,' said Roy. 'Let's find somewhere that you like- and when we do, I'll buy it! Meantime, stay here so that your customers know you're still around.' Now that was an offer I couldn't refuse – and he was very persuasive!

"Finally, one lunchtime, I stumbled on L'Etoile. The walls were bare, but the atmosphere was steeped in history. I thought: 'I've got to take it. Apart from anything else, it's a place to hang my pictures!'"

That history began in the mid 1760's with Charlotte Street, actually commemorating Queen Charlotte who married George III in 1761. A "For Sale" notice was unearthed in the *Morning Chronicle* on April 25 1789.

Described as "a neat and cheerful leasehold house, very desirably situated with detached washhouse and laundry, coach house and stables, lately the residence of a Gentleman", the building remained in private hands until it was bought by the Rossi family at the end of the 19th century.

A notable 18th century resident was Charles Dibdin (1754-1814), singer, novelist, actor and composer – he wrote more than seventy operas – who lived

> **❝ I went to work at the Gay Hussar in Greek Street. The owner and entrepreneur Roy Ackerman was eager to find me a place of my own. 'Come on, Elena,' said Roy. 'Let's find somewhere that you like- and when we do, I'll buy it! ❞**

Elena with her front of house team, (from left) Andreas Thrasyvoulou, Manuel Ramos, Peggy Savage, Costa Panteli and Gerardo Mariscal.

> **❝In more recent times legendary actor Charles Laughton took lodgings on the top floor of No 30.❞**

at the house before moving permanently to Camden Town.

His neighbours included John Constable at No 76, Charlotte Street, while further down the street at No 8 painter Richard Wilson was wielding his brush.

In more recent times legendary actor Charles Laughton took lodgings on the top floor of No 30, and his old desk remained there for many years after his death. By then, L'Etoile was a restaurant.

The actual date can be traced back to 1896 when Frank Rossi and his family started a hostel for waiters in Soho. Mrs Rossi's classic French food was so tasty that

the waiters brought their friends, and in 1904 the Rossis opened the establishment as a full time restaurant. From such humble beginnings, Elena discovered, a star was born. L'Etoile!

Luminaries from Hollywood made a pilgrimage to the doors – urged by word of mouth from their friends back in tinsel town. The likes of Gregory Peck, Rex Harrison, Robert Mitchum, Katharine Hepburn, Elizabeth Taylor, and Ingrid Bergman, as well as home-grown screen legends like Alec Guinness and Richard Attenborough stepped over the threshold.

So did artists and writers such as Augustus John, Dylan Thomas, T.S. Eliot, John Mortimer, Graham Greene and Francis Bacon to add a Bohemian touch to the surroundings. Politicians and the media soon discovered the ambience that remains to this day, while the three private upstairs rooms are regularly used for luncheon and dinner meetings by corporations and even the Booker Prize judges.

Elena greets them all in the same way, which is why they keep coming back. Writing in *The Guardian* recently, Matthew Fort succinctly captured her initial impact. *"She is like a small bird standing at the reception desk, talking on the phone. She is dressed exquisitely in dark grey. Her grey hair clings tightly around her head in marcelled waves. Her eyes are bright behind gold-rimmed spectacles. Her free hand waves expressively.*

At Elena's L'Etoile, celebrating her 'Catey' award for restaurant management from leading trade magazine Caterer and Hotelkeeper with:

1 Longstanding friends George Baker and Lou his wife.

2 Sir Peter Blake, Michael Palin and Roy Ackerman who hosted the party.

3 Burt Kwouk, Lionel Bart and Ned Sherrin.

Elena with her prized collection of
photographs at L'Etoile.

for Elena -

My other mother, & the best & kindest woman in London

Stephen xx

STEPHEN FRY

*She puts the phone down and runs her eye over the tables in the dining
room, as she has been doing for the past sixty years. "Table five," she says to
one of the waiters. "Have you taken their orders yet?"*

That's Elena. Last year (2005) she was officially recognised by
her peers and customers in a ceremony at the Hilton Waldorf
when she was presented with the first ever Homage Award "for
giving service and pleasure to people above what might be
expected in their working life." It was the unanimous decision of a
varied panel of judges ranging from Fay Maschler and Sir Anthony
Joliffe to Ned Sherrin – and each had warm personal recollections
of her.

Probably the high spot in Elena's current tenure at L'Etoile
was the "Oscar" night, still talked about by those fortunate enough
to attend. To mark L'Etoile's centenary in 1996 Elena dedicated the
popular private dining room on the first floor to British winners of
the treasured gold statuette.

In a tribute to Britain's finest film-making talent, she hosted a
party that brought in the likes of Sir John Mills, Sir Sean Connery,

David (Lord) Puttnam

Two of Elena's greatest friends, Melvyn (Lord) Bragg and Ned Sherrin present her with the first 'Homage Award' at the London Waldorf Hotel in 2005.

Lord Attenborough, Jeremy Irons, and Sir Ben Kingsley – Oscar winners all – along with other honoured legends behind the cameras like director John Schlesinger and cinematographic supremos Freddie Young and Jack Cardiff. In all, there were sixteen Oscar winners there that night.

It was also in this room that a group of Fleet Street's top show-business writers threw a luncheon for Lew (Lord) Grade to celebrate the veteran producer's ninetieth birthday. They produced a surprise guest –

Celebrating the Centenary of L'Etoile in 1996 by dedicating its main private dining room to British Oscar Winners.........

1 Elena with Sir John Mills and Sir Sean Connery.

2 Jack Cardiff with his wife Nicki.

3 Aldo chats with Jeremy Irons.

4 Freddie Young with Joan his wife.

Elena's L'Etoile
Centenary Dinner
dedicated to

BRITISH OSCAR WINNERS

Canapés & Champagne Reception

~∞~

Chicken Liver & Wild Mushroom Parfait
served with Hot Brioche

~∞~

Roast Rump of Lamb with a Dauphinoise of Jerusalem
Artichokes and Rosemary Jus

~∞~

Caramelised Banana Cheese Cake

~∞~

Cafe and Friandises

Wines

Mumm, Cordon Rouge NV Champagne

Muscadet de Sèvre-et-Maine
Sauvion, Carte d'Or, tirage sur lie 1995

Château Magnol
Cru Bourgeois, Haut-Médoc 1993

Charles Heidsieck NV Champagne

Ashe Park Mineral Water

for the benefit of
Denville Hall
The Actors' Charitable Trust

★ 30 Charlotte Street, London W1P 1HJ ★
Tel: 0171-636 7189/639 1496

The celebration menu

1 John Schlesinger with Elena.

2 Don Black and his wife, Shirley.

3 Lord and Lady Attenborough with
Sir Ben Kingsley.

Elena and Aldo as Carmen Miranda and George Raft going to George McGhee's Fancy Dress Party in 2002.

Elena partners Lew (Lord) Grade at his 90th birthday party dancing his famous 'Charleston' in the private room dedicated to British Oscar Winners.

Sir Roger Moore and Lew (Lord) Grade compare cigars.

Elena receives her MBE from Prince Charles in 2006.

Sir Roger Moore, who starred in Lew's early hit TV series *The Persuaders*, with Tony Curtis.

At the end of a memorable meal, the pair matched Havana cigars before Lew invited Elena to take the floor with him to dance a lively Charleston.

Behind the scenes, Elena works tirelessly to keep the atmosphere warm, friendly and "special". Seeing herself as mixture of mother hen and mother confessor she tells her thirty-strong staff: "You've got to make everyone feel welcome. Always keep a smile on your face, and don't bring your worries here. It's not good for the business. If you have personal problems, speak to me about it. And they do. They confide in me, and they know I'll listen to them."

Final footnote: when Elena agreed to become restaurant director, Roy Ackerman renamed it Elena's L'Etoile!

The lady herself recalls the moment when she knew about it. "The first I learned of it was when I saw the new menus. There was my name on the cover! It gave me a tremendous shock - but what a compliment. Then I thought to myself: '*That's it. I can't retire now!*'"

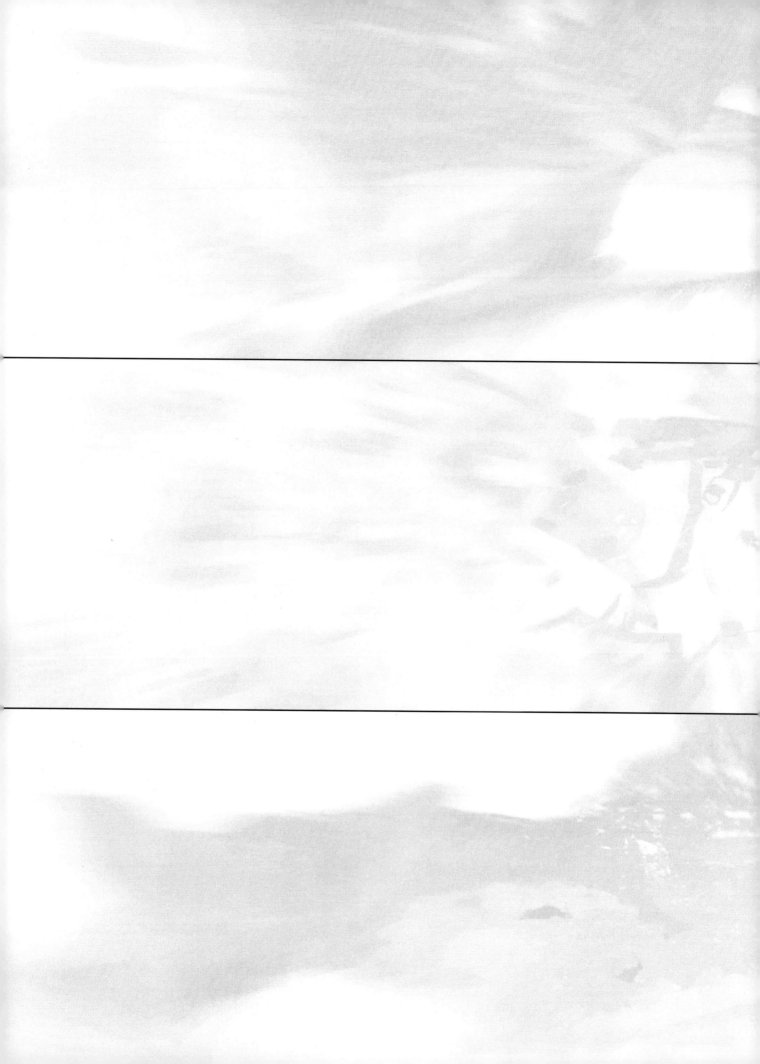

...starters

...mains

...desserts

*See page 198 – Definitions, Sauces, Stocks and Garnishes

Catherine Zeta Jones

I was at L'Escargot. Catherine was in the middle of her hit TV series *The Darling Buds of May*. She came in for lunch with a man who was her agent or manager, and I gave them Table 7 on the first floor, one of the celebrity tables where they could see and be seen. After a bit I couldn't help noticing they were in a heated discussion.

Catherine went off to powder her nose, and as I'm passing their table this man says to me: "Can you believe it Elena?. I'm trying to get her to go to America, to Hollywood, because there may be something there – and she doesn't want to know!"

I say to him: "Really? I can't believe it. Every actress wants to get to Hollywood."

1 at 60th Venice Film Festival 2003

2 with Antonio Banderas in 'Mask of Zorro' 1998

3 with George Clooney in 'Intolerable Cruelty' 2003

4 with husband Michael Douglas at 'Intolerable Cruelty' premier, Los Angeles 2003

5 with Sean Connery at 'Entrapment' photocall, London 1998

6 Press preview of 'Entrapment', Edinburgh 1999

He said: "Neither can I" and gives a hopeless shrug, just as Catherine comes back, sits down and carries on where they'd left off, with a lot of gesturing and head shaking. No one at that time had a hint that Hollywood was beckoning this young teenager from a home grown series like *Darling Buds*.

But I could see the star quality in that girl. She was very beautiful, with a freshness about her that was extraordinary. Even at that age she was turning heads. She had a lovely face and a nice personality. She was fresh and bubbly, and never gave you the feeling of standoffishness.

Eventually of course she did go. And now, every time I see her, I can't help thinking: *My goodness, girl, how you've changed!* She's really acquired the glamour. But let's face it, Britain needs all the glamour girls we can get!

ELENA'S
L'Etoile

39

For Catherine Zeta Jones, Elena recommends...

Croquettes of Salt Cod, Langoustine and Crab with Sweetcorn Butter and Crispy Shallots

...more than meets the eye

Ingredients – serves 4

2 shallots
6 cloves garlic
200ml extra virgin olive oil
225g peeled langoustine
(reserve 3 for garnish)
225g white crab meat
225g salt cod*
pinch cayenne
3 drops lemon juice
3 spring onions
225g Maris Piper potatoes
fish stock*
sweetcorn butter*
rouille*
50g chervil

Method

Croquettes

- Sweat* half the shallots and garlic in extra virgin olive oil until translucent in a large saucepan.
- Add salt cod*– boil for one minute and remove from heat.
- Pan fry langoustine for 2 mins, cool then chop finely.
- Mix crab, langoustine, cod and mashed potato together and season with salt, lemon juice and a little cayenne pepper.
- Mix in finely chopped spring onion tails then mould into small round cakes.

Sweetcorn Butter*

- Wrap one corn-on-the-cob in foil and place in oven at 160C Gas Mark 2-3 for 10-15 mins.
- Strip corn from the other cob and sweat* with remaining shallot and garlic.
- When soft, add wine and vermouth and reduce to syrup.
- Add langoustine stock (see fish stock*) and heat to reduce to three-four tablespoons of liquid.
- Whisk in the cold diced butter, pass through a sieve, add kernels of the second corn-on-the-cob which has been slow oven cooked at 160C Gas Mark 2-3.

Rouille*

- Make rouille* as mayonnaise.
- Season with lemon juice, cayenne and salt.

7

40

Presentation

- Pan fry round cakes and place on a little rouille*.
- Put melted sweetcorn butter* around plate and garnish with three langoustines (shelled and fried).
- Dust shallot rings in flour and deep fry.
- Place deep fried shallots on top of cakes.

Andrew Lloyd Webber

As I was standing at the reception desk at L'Escargot checking the lunchtime list, a gentleman walked up and said: "Good day. I'm with Mr Andrew Lloyd Webber." I was immediately struck by his speaking voice, and as I led him to his table I thought: "What a charming man." Ten out of ten for first impressions! I had no idea who he was, but I sat him down and got him a drink while he waited.

Andrew (now Lord Lloyd Webber) had booked for three, and a few minutes later he arrived with Sarah Brightman, who at that time was his wife, as well as being the star of his much-hyped new show *The Phantom of the Opera*, which was due to open shortly in the West End. He had met Sarah during the run of *Cats*, was stunned by her extraordinary three-octave voice, and composed *Phantom* for her.

"There's a gentleman waiting for you," I told him, took them to the table and left them chatting away with no idea who the guest was. Incidentally, it is not generally known that apart from music, Andrew's other passion is cooking – "especially original pastas," as he confided to me once. "I cook them all the time when I'm at home. It's my speciality!"

After the meal, Andrew's guest stood up and took my hand. He bowed deeply, and said: "Thank you so much. It has been a delight meeting you." And off he went.

I turned to Andrew, and said: "What a wonderful speaking voice that man has."

Andrew replied: "You should hear him sing! You know who he is, don't you?" I had to admit: "No, Andrew, I don't."

"That's Placido Domingo. He's here to help Sarah with her singing for *Phantom*."

I was mortified, but Andrew patted my arm gently. "Don't worry about it, Elena. You can't be expected to recognise everybody."

"Oh but I can," I cried. "That's my job!" I love opera, though I have to confess I prefer dance music to anything else. Remember, I grew up in the days when our main form of entertainment was to go dancing or go to the pictures. Why, I even danced the Charleston with Lew (Lord) Grade when he came to L'Etoile once, in front of the whole restaurant!

But now, whenever I see the Three Tenors, I think back to that day, and the man with the wonderful speaking voice.

1 with his art collection at the Royal Academy, London, 2003

2 Michael Ball opening in 'Aspects of Love in New York 1990

3 Petula Clark in 'Sunset Boulevard' 1996

4 Michael Crawford and Sarah Brightman in 'Phantom of the the Opera

1

3

4

For Andrew Lloyd Webber, Elena recommends...

Lobster Salad with Diced Vegetables and Mayonnaise

...what else for a genius

Method

- Cook the lobster in salted boiling water for 10 mins.
- Place in ice cold water to refresh.
- Dice vegetables, blanch for 5 mins and refresh in ice cold water
- Prepare a plain mayonnaise* by blending three egg yolks and 1 whole egg in a food mixer, then add 1 tblspn French Dijon mustard.
- Slowly pour 100ml extra virgin olive oil to emulsify the eggs.
- Continue blending until mix is thorough and stiff.
- Prepare cooked lobster first by removing the legs.
- Crack the leg shells until it is easy to remove the meat carefully retaining its shape.
- Crack the main shell. Then use a sharp knife to cut in half from head to tail in a straight line. Discard the guts and shell retaining only the flesh.

Ingredients – serves 2

1 x 350g fresh young lobster
100g packet frozen peas
100g carrot
100g turnip
100ml plain mayonnaise*
salt and pepper to season
100g rocket, chervil and
yellow frisée leaves

Presentation

- Drizzle mayonnaise in circle in the centre of a medium sized plate or bowl.
- Reheat the diced vegetables – season with salt and pepper and mix with mayonnaise*.
- Warm the flesh of the lobster in the oven.
- Make a small ring of the vegetable mix.
- Place lobster pieces on top of the vegetable ring.
- Garnish with fresh rocket, chervil and yellow frisée leaves.
- Top the dish with the curved lobster claw.

5

5 Antonio Banderas and
Madonna in 'Evita' 1996

ELENA'S
L'Etoile

Jeremy Irons

2

Jeremy Irons joined the line of Oscar winners queuing – yes, actually queuing, if you can believe that – to join the unforgettable launch of our 'British Oscar Winners' private room at L'Etoile in October 1996. Tall and lean, with those Byronic looks and that wonderful rich voice, he looked every inch the leading man as he arrived in his dinner jacket with his wife Sinead Cusack on his arm.

This remarkable actor had earned his place in our private Hall of Fame with his riveting performance as Count Claus von Bulow, found guilty of attempting to murder his wealthy American wife (Glenn Close) in *Reversal of Fortune*, 1990. I was tempted to ask him how he felt about being likened to "Boris Karloff playing Cary Grant" by one

US critic amid all the flattering reviews, but managed to resist it. I leave that sort of thing
to the critics: after all, they're paid for it, and I'm not! Sparkling Sinead greeted me like
an old friend, which indeed she was: I knew her from visits with her father, the eminent
actor Cyril Cusack, who used to frequent Bianchi's with groups of other young actors,
as well as her brothers Padraig and Paul, for after-show late-night theatre parties.

Jeremy could appear a little aloof until you got to know him, but once he relaxed
he was the most entertaining of guests, full of the kind of anecdotes he swapped that
night at L'Etoile with Sean Connery and his wife Micheline in the restaurant over dinner
after the grand opening.

5 in 'Casanova' 2005

6 in 'Being Julia' in 2004

Ingredients – serves 4-6

1kg field mushrooms, sliced
1 small onion, finely sliced
1 leek (white part only)
finely sliced
50g butter
750ml chicken stock*
1 tablespoon flour
250ml Madeira
1 bay leaf
1 small bunch thyme
1 bunch chervil
2 tspns truffle oil

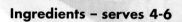

Method
- Sweat* onion and leek in butter in a large saucepan until translucent Add mushrooms, bay leaf and thyme until nearly all moisture has evaporated, then add flour.
- Cook on medium heat for 3 mins, then add Madeira and chicken stock*.
- Cook on medium heat for further 15 mins.
- Liquidise soup and strain through a coarse sieve.

Presentation
- To serve – warm the soup, pour into bowls.
- Sprinkle a little truffle oil on top.
- Add a few chervil leaves.

49

Judi Dench

That marvellous actress Judi Dench was another regular at my restaurants, and I was thrilled when she became a Dame. Despite her austere performances as Queen Victoria and even "M" in the James Bond films, I can assure you there's nothing of the "grand dame" about her. Judi is warm, funny, and lovely company.

One evening she and her actor husband Michael Williams booked a table for eight at L'Escargot to celebrate their daughter Finty's fourteenth birthday with a party of school friends. That meant no alcohol, of course. The impresario Harold Prince came in, and spotted them across the room. He beckoned me over. "Elena, would you take a bottle of champagne over, but don't say who sent it!"

I told him: "They don't want any drinks on that table." But he insisted, so I went over with a bottle of champagne. Michael spotted Harold, who then joined them. In the end they gave all the children a sip or two of bubbly. And they all had a lovely evening.

Next time I saw Judi, she said: "Elena! You know what you did that night? Well, none of those girls could go to school next morning – they were still sozzled!"

I said: "Please don't blame me! It was all Harold Prince's fault."

1 as 'M' in the James Bond film
'Tomorrow Never Dies' 1997

2 with her Oscar for 'Elizabeth 1' in
Los Angeles 1999

3 with Kelly Reilly in 'Mrs Henderson
Presents' 2005

For Judi Dench, Elena recommends...

Chicory & Asparagus Salad with Poached Egg, Chorizo and Croutons

...healthy can be indulgent

Ingredients – serves 4

Salad
2 heads Belgium endive sliced
length ways
1 x 500g bunch green asparagus,
mixed leaves of oak, rocket and
yellow frisée
4 poached eggs
100g chorizo,
2 slices of bread cut into small squares
and fried in butter
100g croutons*
½ bunches chervil
vinaigrette (mustard)*

4 in 'Mrs Brown' 1997

5 in 'Chocolat' 2000

Method
- Blanch asparagus and cut in half.
- Cut chorizo into small squares and pan fry
  in a little oil.
- Dress and season chicory and asparagus
  with the mustard vinaigrette.
- Place in a criss-cross on the middle
  of the plate, with a small pile of
  dressed leaves.
- Poach eggs and keep hot.

Presentation
- Place poached eggs on top of leaves.
- Spoon some chorizo and a little oil
  (from the chorizo) over the eggs.
- Scatter some croutons over the salad.
- Finish with chervil.

1 'Oh What a Lovely War' 1969

2 with Michael Caine in 'Wrong Box' 1966

3 with Mary

4 with Valerie Hobson in 'Great Expectations' 1946

John Mills

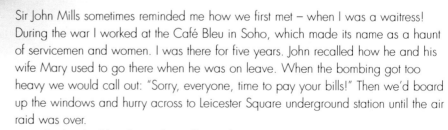

Sir John Mills sometimes reminded me how we first met – when I was a waitress!
During the war I worked at the Café Bleu in Soho, which made its name as a haunt
of servicemen and women. I was there for five years. John recalled how he and his
wife Mary used to go there when he was on leave. When the bombing got too
heavy we would call out: "Sorry, everyone, time to pay your bills!" Then we'd board
up the windows and hurry across to Leicester Square underground station until the air
raid was over.

John has had his share of war films, of course. He has probably played more
screen heroes than any other actor – his performance as *Scott of the Antarctic* still
moves me to tears. But unlike some stars he never takes the part home with him –
away from the screen he is the most courteous and unassuming person you'll ever

meet. It's only when you see him in films that you realise what a wonderful actor he is.

John likes to talk food. "Elena," he says, "I've never bothered with a diet. There's no need, if you're careful. Mary and I never have two heavy meals in one day. I'll have a salad lunch, which leaves plenty of room for the evening.

"If I do the cooking at home, I have one dish I do splendidly. It's my famous salmon cutlet. I marinate it for 75 minutes in sunflower oil, adding black pepper, lemon juice and chopped onion. I keep turning the fish over for more than an hour so the juice goes right through. Then I grill them, five minutes each side and then another two so that they get seven minutes each. The result is absolutely fabulous!" And Mary? "She can rustle up wonderful scrambled eggs!"

"You must meet Kevin," I tell him. "If he needs any help, I know where to look."

Ingredients – serves 2

50g butter
2 cloves garlic
400ml chicken stock*
2 tbsp double cream
100g dried, soaked Arborio
(risotto) rice
100g dried cep mushrooms,
finely sliced
1 white Spanish onion
150g Parmesan
small bunch chives
small bunch parsley
salt and freshly ground
black pepper
extra virgin olive oil
50g fresh asparagus

Method

Risotto

- Melt half the butter in a heavy pan.
- Add chopped onion with chopped heads of garlic to sweat* the onions colourless.
- When the onions have softened add finely sliced mushrooms and rice to the pan, cook for a further 2-3 mins.
- Meanwhile heat the chicken stock until simmering. Add 2 ladles of stock to the rice mixture. Adjust heat to simmering, and stir. Continue to add the stock until it has been absorbed by the rice.
- When rice is 'al dente'* and the texture is creamy (process is about 10 mins) season with salt and pepper and finish with the double cream.

Parmesan Crust

- Take 100g Parmesan.
- Add to 25ml chicken stock to make a paste.
- Add knob of unsalted butter.
- Mix in a bowl.
- Take an upturned cake tin approx 9 ins diameter.
- Cover with greaseproof paper and rub with oil.
- Use piping bag to make small circles (5cm) of the Parmesan mix across the tin. For best effect use more mix on one side.
- Bake in oven at 220C Gas Mark 7 for 2 mins.

John Mills lets George Peppard know about the dangers he will face after parachuting into enemy territory.
Metro-Goldwyn-Mayer presents "OPERATION CROSSBOW" in Panavision and Metrocolor

For John Mills, Elena recommends...

Mushroom Risotto with Parmesan Gallete and Truffle Oil

...and holding hands with Mary

Presentation

- Stir chopped chives and parsley and add a little grated Parmesan through the risotto.
- Carefully release the crust from the upturned cake tin where the melted Parmesan will have created a flat base with a half shell effect.
- Place risotto mix in the Parmesan crust and serve immediately.
- Blanch asparagus for 3 mins in salted boiling water. Use tips as garnish.

ELENA'S
L'Etoile

Faye Dunaway

Faye Dunaway is the archetypal movie star. When I was running Bianchi's she was at the height of her fame, with *Bonnie and Clyde* a massive success, and the world at her feet. I was always amused to see how she arrived – hidden in a cloak with dark glasses and a huge hat over her face so no-one could identify her. Didn't she realise that when people spot someone like that they naturally gawp to see who's under the hat!

But after a few visits she finally realised that nobody was going to bother her, and relaxed visibly. She even took her hat off. The night I won't forget is when she came in for dinner with her photographer husband Terry O'Neill, prior to going over to Ronnie Scott's jazz club afterwards. Bianchi's seemed to be a stepping stone for people going on to a late-night jazz session there. Terry had an impressive watch on his wrist, a bulky timepiece that he showed me with some pride. It was a real beauty. "This is my father's watch, Elena. It was given to him by the railways when he retired."

After dinner they got up and left, and I cleared away their table as I sometimes did to help out the staff. I was back at the reception desk – and all of a sudden there was Faye at my elbow, with panic written all over her. "Terry left his watch on the table," she cried. "I've come back for it!" I looked blankly at her.

"There's no watch here," I told her. "I cleared the table myself. No-one else has gone near it. And no way would anyone have picked that watch up, because I would have seen it." This sort of thing can be very embarrassing, a watch going missing, or for that matter any customer thinking something has been stolen. But Faye was saying wildly: "It must be here. He's so upset."

I faced her. "Where is he?"

"Over at Ronnie Scott's."

"Come on," I said firmly. "I'll go with you." And with that I went down to the street, marched across the road, and walked straight into the jazz club to find Terry.

"Listen," I said. "I know you took your watch off, but I'm sure you put it back on again...You put it on your wrist."

The ace photographer looked down, rolled up his jacket sleeve – and went red. "Oh my God, here it is!" They stared at each other. "I'm so sorry..."

"That's all right," I said. "These things happen. Next time wear short sleeves!" Yet again, diplomacy saves the day!

1 in 'The Thomas Crown Affair' 1968

2 in 'Casanova' 1987

3 with Warren Beatty as 'Bonnie and Clyde' in 1967

6

4 in 'Network' 1976

5 at the BAFTA Awards 2000

Method

- Roll beef tightly in clingfilm and place in freezer finely sliced.
- Trim fennel, retain fronds at end.
- Slice very finely and place in iced water.
- Brush 4 x 10 inch plates with a little extra virgin olive oil.
- Slice meat very finely and overlap neatly on the plate.

Presentation

- Drop small flakes of cheese on each plate, then some fennel slices that have been dressed in extra virgin olive oil.
- Grind black pepper liberally and sprinkle fronds of fennel over the dish.
- Finally, add dressed rocket and finely sliced red onion to the middle of each plate.

Ingredients – serves 4

200g middle cut fillet of beef
½ red onion
100g Roquefort cheese
80g rocket leaves

For Faye Dunaway, Elena recommends...

Carpaccio of Beef with Rocket, Red Onion & Roquefort

...looks too good to eat

Robert Redford

Suddenly there he was – Robert Redford, walking down the centre aisle of L'Etoile to his table, sitting down, taking off a peaked cap to show his thick thatch of fair hair, now streaked with grey...and not a single person in the restaurant noticed him. Oh, apart from one couple, who beckoned me over. "Is that – is that – ?" they stuttered. "Yes, it is," I said, before they could complete the sentence.

To be honest, I was as dumbfounded as they were. The table had been reserved in another name, for a party of four, and I had no idea Hollywood's 'golden boy' was in town. But he took off his tinted glasses to study the menu, and seemed at home immediately. They were an animated group, and after a lively lunch they got up to leave. I shook his hand, and suddenly heard myself saying: "Mr Redford, when are you going to make another film?" He paused, looked me in the eye with that steady blue gaze, and responded: "Quite honestly, I don't know." "Well," I told him firmly. "Just make sure it isn't full of chases and car crashes!"

The truth is that although he doesn't go in for that kind of thing too much, every Hollywood film I see today seems to have car chases and crashes, and it all becomes terribly boring. He gave me a broad grin, the kind of boyish smile that used to make girls go weak at the knees, and said quietly: "All right, Elena. If that's how you feel – I won't!" What a charmer that man is!

1 with Paul Newman in 'Butch Cassidy and the Sundance Kid' 1969

2 in 'The Great Gatsby' 1974

3 with Scarlett Johansson in 'The Horse Whisperer' 1973

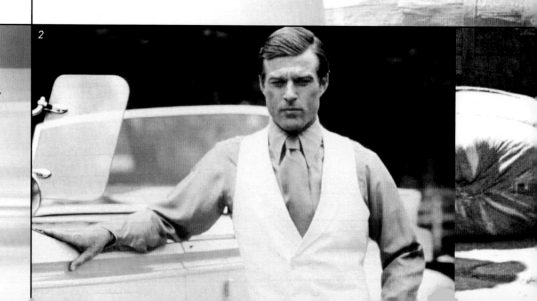

2

Ingredients – serves up to 10

1kg Mozzarella block
100ml extra virgin olive oil
1 bunch fresh basil
12 vine tomatoes
1 terrine mould approx
30 cm long
200g yellow frisée and
rocket leaves
salt and pepper

Method

- Blanch the 12 vine tomatoes for 30 seconds in boiling water.
- Cut and peel tomatoes into halves.
- Slice1k block Mozzarella into three slices (long ones).
- Cover the terrine mould with cling film, and make sure the film is fitted firmly, from top to bottom.
- Place the halves of tomatoes on the bottom of the mould, add some green leaves of fresh basil, drizzle olive oil, season with salt and pepper Place long Mozzarella slice on top.
- Repeat the process until the mould is full.
- Finish the last layer with tomato halves and press hard on the whole mould.
- Leave the tomato mozzarella terrine to chill in fridge for 24 hours, prior to serving.

Presentation

- Slice a good portion, using a long sharp knife.
- Place the portion on a flat plate, and garnish with some leaves of fresh rocket and yellow frisée.
- Drizzle olive oil on top and around the plate.
- Elena's Tomato Mozzarella Terrine can be served as a starter or main course.

4 with Barbra Streisand in 'The Way We Were' 1973

5 with Jack Warden in 'All the President's Men' 1976

6 with Meryl Streep filming 'Out of Africa' 1985

For Robert Redford, Elena recommends...

Elena's Tomato and Mozzarella Terrine

...divine looks and content to match

Sarah Ferguson

Sarah Ferguson's bright red hair is an eye-catcher, and the Duchess of York herself has always been a head-turner whenever she comes into any of my restaurants. Sarah Ferguson is also a great one for fund-raising, and she has never stopped pulling my leg over the way I raised money for a charity called The Sick Children's Fund. This involves homes where relatives with children in hospital can stay rather than travel up to London every day from out of town to visit them.

It's a marvellous idea, and when I first heard about them I visited a house personally in Gray's Inn Road. I was so impressed that I decided to get involved in helping them.

I got my chance unexpectedly when a customer in L'Escargot casually asked me one lunchtime how many miles I actually walked in a day? I said I had no idea. A week later she was in again – and this time brought a pedometer with her! "Let's find out, Elena."

I wasn't sure how to fix the thing on, but after toying around with it I came up with the idea of hooking it on to a black lace garter which I made specially and wore above my right knee! Saucy? Well, it wasn't quite the Moulin Rouge but I can tell you that on that first day I did ten miles! And that was just walking around the building at lunch and dinner.

Right, I thought. *I'll do a charity walk.* Next day I put on this contraption again, and went as usual from table to table. Someone noticed a strange sound. "What's that clicking noise, Elena? Are you bugging our table?" Well, it certainly wasn't my joints!

I said: "No, I'm doing a charity walk." And pulled up my skirt to show them the pedometer attached above my knee! I couldn't go out and jog, so I kept it strictly to my day's work inside L'Escargot. Tick-tick-tick it went.

On an impulse, I announced: "I can average 50 miles in a week." To which the answer was a resounding: "You'll never do that!" Next thing, we were talking money. "If you want to put money on it, you can do it by the mile, say ten pence a mile?"

The idea caught fire. I put up a big board on the wall, writing in the names and bets. Forget ten pence! Most people gave me one pound a mile, and we did it for a month. In the week that counted I notched up 53 miles, Monday to Friday. No wonder I'm so fit.

At the end of the month, I had accumulated £9,000.50p., and I was as amazed as anyone. The fact is, I've got loads of grandchildren, all of them healthy, thank God, and I really wanted to do something for these poor kids who were ill in hospital.

Sarah Ferguson is patron of that charity. When I met her and told how I'd raised it, she threw back here head and laughed out loud. "I've never heard anything like it, Elena," she said.

"Nor have I," I replied, reaching into my handbag. "But here's the cheque to prove it!"

2

1 taking tea with Wedgwood in New York

2 at the premiere party for 'The White
Countess' London, 2006

1

For Sarah Ferguson, Elena recommends...

Warm Potato and Horseradish Pancake with Wild Smoked Salmon and Lemon Butter

...an infectious personality

Ingredients – serves 4

300g wild smoked salmon
250g Maris Piper potatoes
2 tspn flour
2 whole eggs
2 yolks
2 whites (whisked)
50ml double cream
1 tblspn freshly grated
horseradish

Method

- Mash all ingredients except salmon together in bowl.
- Take four small non-stick blini pans (13cm/5 ins), pour a little oil inside.
- Heat to almost smoking, then pour in 13mm (½ in.) of mix.
- Leave on flame for 30 seconds, then transfer to a medium grill, and cook top of pancakes for 5 mins.
- Alternatively, oven bake at 180C Gas Mark 4 for 5-7 mins.
- Leave to cool for five mins in pan, then turn out on to warmed plate.

Presentation

- Fold some salmon neatly on top, and surround with a little lemon and chive butter*, or with wedges of lemon and lashings of black pepper.
- Top with whipped double cream.

3 at the Giorgio Armani Gala at the Royal Academy, London, 2003

4 at Veuve Clicquot polo event 2004

David Lean

Sir David Lean had a fearsome reputation among actors and film crews, but I never saw any of it in the many times he came to L'Escargot.

When he first walked in, and I recognised him, I have to admit I felt a twinge of apprehension. Here was a giant of the cinema, and his reputation had preceded him. Was this the man who had survived the jungles of Sri Lanka to make *Bridge on the River Kwai* or the heat of North Africa for *Lawrence of Arabia*? Both masterpieces, with a wealth of awards – and, of course, many other films besides. It was hard to believe, as I ushered him to his table and took his order, that this sturdy, dark-eyed figure in sports jacket and slacks was one of the cinema's truly towering icons.

He would usually be with a group of business types for luncheon meetings, but in the evenings he would appear with his lovely wife – one of six, and quite honestly I'm not sure which one it was, except that she was dark-haired and exotic! They would fly in from their villa in the South of France.

The last time I saw him he had just finished making *A Passage to India*, and I remember wishing him good luck with the Academy Awards. "Thank you, Elena, " he said gravely. "We always hope for the best." That year (1984), it was not to be. The film had an amazing nine nominations – but was pipped at the post for the big prizes by *Amadeus*, which won Oscars for best film and best director for Milos Forman. But Sir David, as he became, took it with a shrug. After all, he had enough awards overflowing his mantelpiece to last him a lifetime.

1 filming 'A Passage to India' 1984

2 Peter O'Toole in 'Lawrence of Arabia' 1962

3 Alec Guinness and Sessue Hayakawa in 'The Bridge on the River Kwai' 1957

Ingredients – serves up to 12

500g chicken livers
650g unsalted butter melted and
kept at 55C
250g foie gras
4 whole eggs
4 yolks
100ml Armagnac
150ml port
100ml Madeira
3 chopped shallots
3 cloves of garlic, chopped
½ bunch thyme, chopped
1 bay leaf
1 tblspn castor sugar
200g mixed leaves – rocket
and yellow frisée
240g cornichons – baby
pickled cucumbers
choice of organic country
loaf or brioche

Method

- Sweat* shallots and garlic in a little butter.
- Add thyme, bay leaf, sugar and all alcohol.
- Reduce by ½, take off heat and cool.
- Clean livers and foie gras. Pour alcoholic mix over them.
- Add eggs and yolks to mixture.
- Blend liver mix in liquidiser and pass through sieve.
- Pre-heat oven to 140C Gas Mark 1.
- Butter 1 terrine mould (½ litre size).
- Place liver mix back in liquidiser and start slow blend.
- Remove cap from the top, and add the melted butter in a steady stream, season well with salt and a generous amount of white pepper.
- Pour mix into terrine. Place into a water bath, then into oven, and cook for 45-60mins at 140C Gas Mark 1.
- When parfait is cooled it will be slightly firm on the side – and wobbly in the middle.
- Remove parfait from terrine and coat completely with clarified butter.
- Wrap in cling film and place in fridge for 2 hours.

Presentation

- To serve, put a few mixed leaves at the top of the plate, and a slice of parfait in the centre. Serve with cornichons and organic country loaf or toasted brioche.

4 with Omar Sharif filming 'Dr Zhivago' 1965

5 filming 'A Passage to India' 1984

For David Lean, Elena recommends...

Smooth Chicken Liver & Foie
Gras Parfait with Armagnac

...sooth sophistication

Terry Wogan

Sir Terry Wogan is a one-man charm offensive on legs. To hear him at the Eurovision Song Contest you might think he has something of a caustic turn of phrase, a roguish Irish mischief-maker – and of course you'd be right. Otherwise what a dull affair the Eurovision would be. But this is his public persona, switched on like a light bulb for his annual excursion into the dark arts of the song festival. I exaggerate, of course.

Terry, who always likes his favourite table in the window when he dines at L'Etoile, looks forward to this challenge with more relish than he lets on. And in person, he is a delight. Customers who pass by on their way in or out of the restaurant and pause to say hullo are always greeted with a cheery word in reply. Not for him the stuck-up or the pompous. Terry knows his public, and leaves everyone with a smile on their face to pass the word around what a good guy he is. Take my word for it: with the wickedly witty Mr Wogan, what you see is what you get!

1 with 'himself' at the Royal Society
of Portrait Painters exhibition
1993

2 with Ulrika Jonsson for the
'Eurovision Song Contest' 1998

3 at Sony Radio Awards 2001

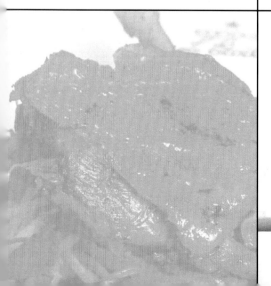

2

1

3

★

ELENA'S

L'Etoile

For Terry Wogan, Elena recommends...

Crispy Duck Salad with Soy Dressing and Pickled Ginger

...always in fashion

Ingredients – serves 4

4 x 6oz duck legs trimmed
300ml duck fat
pinch Malden sea salt
pinch Chinese five spice

Salad
100g sushi ginger
1 cucumber cut into strips
1 bunch watercress
5 spring onions
1 bunch chopped coriander
½ mouli (chinese white radish)
2 x 100g carrots

Dressing
100ml vegetable oil
25ml soy sauce
25ml balsamic vinegar
1-star anise – infuse with
zest of 1 lemon
1 bunch coriander

Method
Duck
- Sprinkle one good pinch of Malden sea salt and 1 pinch of Chinese five spice on the duck legs.
- Rub in, and leave for 12 hrs.
- Place legs in a pan, cover with duck fat and cover with a lid.
- Place in oven on 60C Gas Mark ½ for 2-3 hrs, or until the thigh bone can easily be twisted out of the duck leg. Leave legs to cool in the fat.
- When cool place on a wire rack, cover protruding shin bone with foil.
- Place legs in fridge.

Method
Dressing
- Whisk ingredients together in a bowl.
- Cut cucumber, mouli and carrot into long strips on a Japonaise mandolin slicer but slice spring onions by hand.

Presentation
- Drizzle extra virgin olive oil an oven-proof pan and heat until smoking
- Place duck legs in, skin side down.
- Colour a little, then place in a hot oven 200-220C Gas Mark 6-7 for 12 mins.
- Take out, turn skin side up and leave on the side.
- Mix all salad ingredients: carrots, mouli, cucumber, coriander, watercress and pickled ginger.
- Dress with soy dressing.
- Place in middle of plate in a neat pile, and place duck leg on top.
- Brush some dressing over the duck leg, and spoon a little dressing around the plate.

4

5

4 back at BBC Radio 2 in 1993 –
with two alarm clocks

5 as Pudsey Bear for 'BBC Children
in Need' 1995

Cameron Mackintosh

Sir Cameron Mackintosh's secretary rang one evening. "Elena, can you send round a big bowl of chips – enough for ten people? They've been to a birthday party, and all they want is a bowl of your chips." I don't do this sort of thing often. But Cameron's Really Useful Company is round the corner from the L'Etoile, and chips are our speciality anyway – we make them large and beautifully crisp on the outside, and they go down a treat.

Also, Cameron and I go back a long way – all the way back to the days of Bianchi's when he was a poorly paid and frequently out-of-work young actor. I once saw him sweeping the stage of the Drury Lane Theatre during the run of *Hello, Dolly!* when I happened to be in the Royal Box as guest of one of my customers, so I had a bird's eye view of him wielding the broom before the show. Cameron had fallen in love with the theatre at a very early age, and would do anything to be close to the footlights. In those days he used to come into Bianchi's and have the cheapest thing on the menu – a bowl of soup and a plate of spaghetti.

Now here he is, a multi-millionaire impresario…and still wanting a bowl of chips. So I had a huge ramekin of chips prepared, a car was waiting outside, and we were just about to load up when the phone rang again. Cameron himself this time: "Don't bother, Elena. We've changed our minds, and we're all coming to the restaurant." Then, as an afterthought: "Have you got room?" I had, just, squeezing them in around two tables at the back when they all came pouring in, several sheets to the wind.

"Don't go to too much trouble," Cameron said. "We'll have fishcakes all round. Oh – and chips."

"Of course," I said. The other lot were stone cold by now, and they'd had to be thrown away.

"You're a star," he told me as they all tucked in. "If I could get you into all my shows I'd have a success in every one!" How can you resist a smooth talker like that?

A few days later he was in again, and handed me an envelope. I thought he was giving me an advert for one of his shows, and didn't even open it until I got home. Then my jaw dropped. Inside were two first-class tickets for myself and Aldo on the Orient Express to Venice, with three days at the famous Danielli Hotel on the Grand Canal. When we walked into the suite, there was an enormous bunch of roses and a bowl full of exotic fruits awaiting us, along with a bottle of champagne. Plus a note: "Have a wonderful time!" We raised a Bellini to a very generous friend.

Actually, Cameron had found out it was my birthday. So it wasn't just a thank you for the chips.

1 & 2 *'Cats' on tour in Moscow, 2005*

3 *with Andrew Lloyd Webber who presented Cameron with a London Routemaster Bus when 'Les Miserables' moved from the Palace Theatre to the Queen's Theatre in 2004.*

4 *at the premiere party for 'Moulin Rouge' 2001*

For Cameron Mackintosh, Elena recommends...

Seared Scallops withSmoked Bacon and Celeriac Purée, Sauce Bercy

...he just loves scallops

Ingredients – serves 2

4 fresh King scallops – on
the shell
100g celeriac (root of a
celery plant)
50ml milk
2 rashers sliced streaky bacon
pinch salt
knob of butter
zest of 1 lemon
1 shallot
1 bunch parsley
2 tspns double cream

Method
Celeriac puree
- Peel the celeriac, place in a small saucepan in a 50/50 mix of water and milk, lightly salted on medium heat.
- Stir until soft like mashed potato.
- Pass through a sieve, add butter and lemon zest, with salt, pepper and cream to create celeriac puree as a base for the scallops.

Method
Scallops
- Slice scallops sideways into 1 cm slices. Heat pan until smoking.
- Season scallops both sides with salt.
- Paint some clarified butter on the scallops with a pastry brush and pan fry to seal on a very high heat for 25-30 secs each side.
- Scallops are best medium rare.

Presentation
- Serve scallops and roe if present, on a bed of celeriac puree with a Sauce Bercy* (white wine sauce from Burgundy with chopped shallots, chopped parsley and cream reduction sauce).
- Pour sauce round edge of plate – it's very white but with an attractive green tint.
- Finally, add crispy bacon on the top.

5 Sarah Brightman and Michael Crawford in 'Phantom of the Opera' at Her Majesty's Theatre, London, 2004

6 Phantom of the Opera 1991 Her Majesty's Theatre, London

5

6

Maria Callas

1 with her poodles in 1969

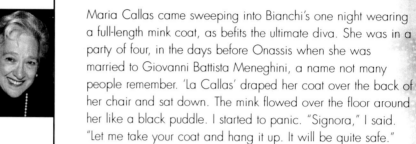

Maria Callas came sweeping into Bianchi's one night wearing a full-length mink coat, as befits the ultimate diva. She was in a party of four, in the days before Onassis when she was married to Giovanni Battista Meneghini, a name not many people remember. 'La Callas' draped her coat over the back of her chair and sat down. The mink flowed over the floor around her like a black puddle. I started to panic. "Signora," I said. "Let me take your coat and hang it up. It will be quite safe."

But she waved an imperious hand. "Leave it. Leave it there!" The whole restaurant was riveted, all eyes upon this legend in our midst.

I said unhappily: "But someone may step on it. Or worse, spill something over it. You would be very angry if a bowl of minestrone was upset over that beautiful coat." It was a potentially disastrous situation. Try and get a red wine stain out of a mink coat!

"Angry!" Those huge hypnotic dark eyes flashed fire. "Of course I would be angry. Just make sure it doesn't happen."

Somehow we got through the night without her mink coat coming to any harm. The waiters walked on eggs around that coat. Any customer who approached it was discreetly steered away. At the end I drew a deep breath of relief. No drips, no spillage. Not even a footprint.

Tempting though it was, I was far too polite to suggest she sang for her supper.

ELENA'S
*
L'Étoile

Ingredients – serves 2

250g puff pastry
1 bunch medium asparagus
hollandaise sauce*
50g chopped parsley
50g chervil

Method

- Roll out the puff pastry to a rectangle 5mm thick.
- Cut into smaller rectangles strips about 2cm width.
- Add stripes to the pastry using a knife leaving cut side uppermost.
- Bake the pastry strips in the oven at 220C Gas mark 7 for 15-17 mins.
- Place the asparagus into salted boiling water for 3-4 mins maximum.
- Allow to cool to retain colour – then refresh in iced water.

Presentation

- Reheat rolled pastry rectangles and the asparagus.
- Place baked pastry strips on a warm flat plate.
- Position asparagus on the pastry strips all in same direction.
- Drizzle the hollandaise sauce* on top of the asparagus.
- Place another strip of baked pastry on top and garnish with fresh chervil and parsley.

2 greeting admirers after performing at Theatre des Champs Elysee, Paris, 1973

Feuillete Asparagus

...an iconic presence

John Gielgud

I nearly died the night Sir John Gielgud walked in to L'Escargot – unannounced, without any booking. It was a Friday, and we had been booked solid. How could I turn this noble theatrical knight away? By a stroke of luck I had one table left – but in the middle of the room upstairs, the last place he would have wanted to sit. Someone had cancelled. Most celebrities, as you might guess, prefer tables away from the limelight, especially if they have someone with them whom they wish to keep discreet.

Gielgud was with Charles Surridge, the director of *Brideshead Revisited*. I still remember him as the reclusive father Edward Ryder (Jeremy Irons played his son Charles) in the award-winning TV series based on Evelyn Waugh's novel. When the two of them came into the reception area, I cried: "Oh, my God! I've only got one table left – in the middle of the room." To which Sir John declaimed in that wonderful

voice: "That will be quite all right, my dear. I never mind being centre-stage!" And the pair of them happily followed me upstairs, and sat down with all eyes upon them.

At the end of their meal, Sir John looked at me with a twinkle and said: "My dear, isn't it wonderful to be in a dining room where the young and the old are enjoying the same atmosphere." Wasn't that nice! No-one troubled him, no-one asked him for an autograph.

In fact, I don't allow it. If someone approaches me, I'm very firm. "No," I tell them. "If you want to get the celebrity outside after they've left, that's all right. But not at the table."

But Sir John seemed to relish it. He is one of the few, I suspect, who would have signed for every table in the house!

1 rehearsing 'Julius Caesar' in 1953 with Deborah Kerr, Louis Calhern, Marlon Brando, James Mason and Edmund O'Brien

2 with James Mason in 'Julius Caesar' 1953

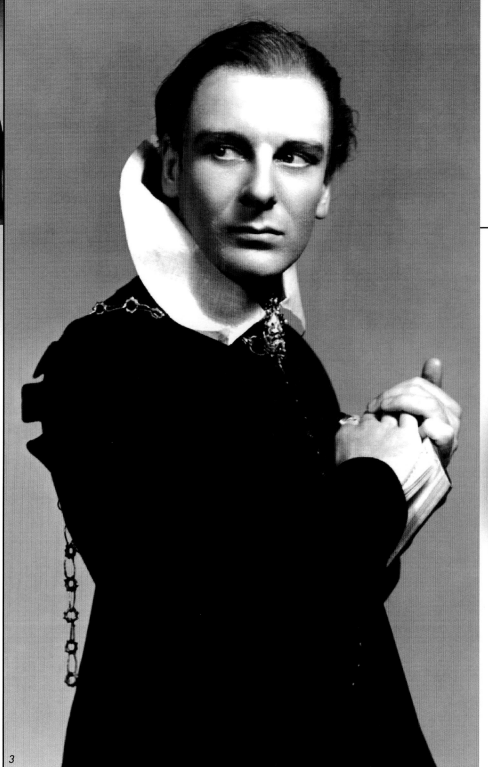

3 as 'Hamlet' in 1936

4 with Noel Coward in 'Around the World in 80 Days' 1956

5 with Ralph Richardson in 'Eagle in a Cage' 1972

Ingredients – serves 4

500g mixed fish (red mullet-weaver and gurnard – scaled) chopped (gutted), heads and all.
300g tinned tomatoes
300ml white wine
500ml water
1 star anis
1 tbspn tomato puree
100g chopped carrots
1 chopped onion
1 chopped leek
2 sticks celery
½ garlic clove
50ml olive oil
1 bay leaf
small bunch thyme
pinch of cayenne
Herbs de Provence

Method
- Sweat* vegetables in olive oil for 30 mins in a large pan.
- Add fish and tomato puree and cook for 15 mins on medium heat.
- Add wine and reduce mix by half.
- Add tin of tomatoes, bay and thyme, star anis, a good pinch of Herbs de Provence, salt, cayenne and 500ml of water.
- Bring to the boil and simmer for further 30 mins.
- Pass through a vegetable mouli into a blender and liquidise to emulsify the soup.
- Pass through a strainer to remove bones and season to taste.

For John Gielgud, Elena recommends...

Fish Soup with Croutons and Garlic Mayonnaise

...not for the faint hearted

Presentation
- Serve with croutons* and garlic mayonnaise.

Mick Jagger

How does Sir Mick Jagger stay so thin? It must be all those calories he burns off at his Rolling Stones concerts, I thought to myself, as he appeared at L'Escargot one day for lunch with his then wife, the exotic Bianca, unannounced and without a booking. Oh, dear. The place was full to bursting, and I had to tell him: "I'm sorry, but there's only one table left, and it's in the centre of the room."

These things matter a lot. I thought that like most of the scores of celebrities I've welcomed into my restaurants he would want a discreet table at the side or, better still, in a corner away from curious eyes. But no. Mick, speaking for both of them, said: "That's okay with us. Put us anywhere you can." He took his place smack in the middle of the packed room on the main floor.

He came back a week later, this time with his daughter Jade, a teenager blossoming into the beauty she has since become. And guess what? He'd booked ahead, and this time actually asked for the same table again. Everyone has their favourite table at restaurants, and if they're wise they get the number from the waiter before they leave and make sure they ask for it again next time. Mick was no exception. He asked for the same table every time he came. But I should mention at this point that our centre table was *not* in the spotlight as you might imagine but actually had two columns on either side which gave it a certain privacy of its own. From then on Mick came regularly with either Bianca or Jade, while Bianca came with either Mick or Jade – but never in a threesome. I would love to have seen them as a family group, but it never happened.

At least they kept coming, and I found Mick warm, witty and humorous, far removed from his raunchy stage image that kept the fans squealing. He tucked into his pasta with a vengeance – but still remained as thin as a rake. Don't ask me how he did it. All I know is that if I'd been his mother, I'd have been worried sick!

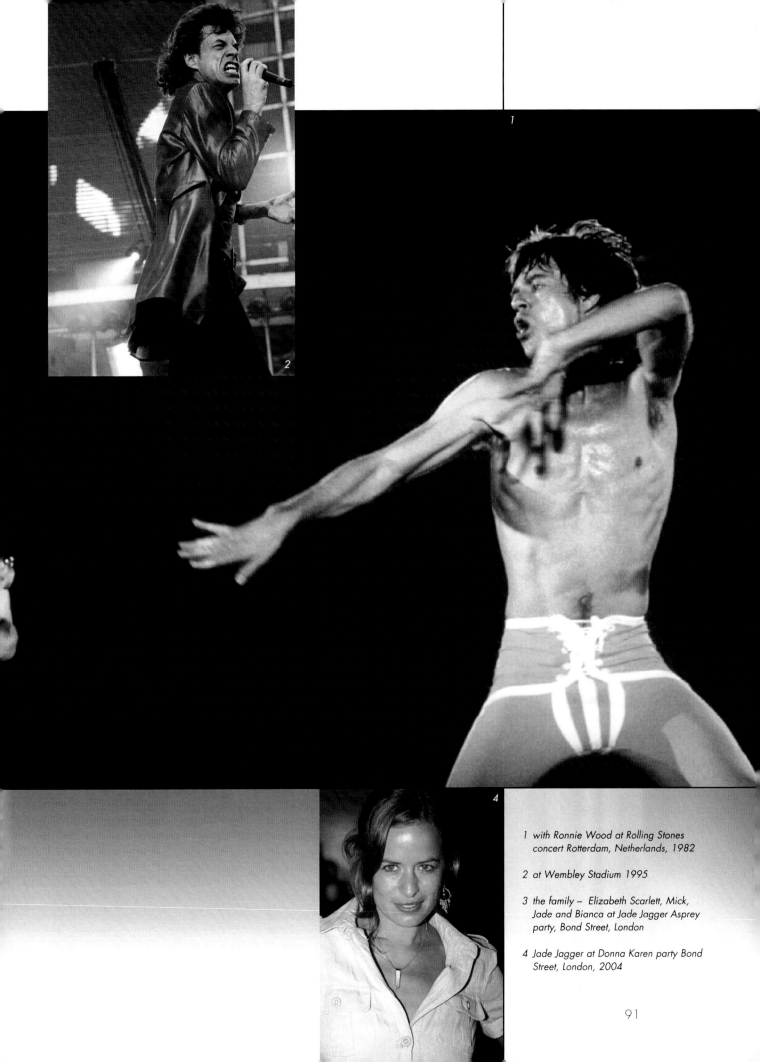

1 with Ronnie Wood at Rolling Stones
  concert Rotterdam, Netherlands, 1982

2 at Wembley Stadium 1995

3 the family – Elizabeth Scarlett, Mick,
  Jade and Bianca at Jade Jagger Asprey
  party, Bond Street, London

4 Jade Jagger at Donna Karen party Bond
  Street, London, 2004

Ingredients – serves 4

4 x 150/20g centre cut
pieces of English fillet
of beef
100g button mushrooms
4 x 60g slices fresh foie gras
4 x 5in. puff pastry circles
1 chopped shallot
25g butter
25g truffle

Method

- Sweat* shallots in butter in a small saucepan until translucent.
- Add mushrooms, season and cook until soft, then blend in a food mixer.
- Add a few drops of truffle juice or chopped truffle to this mix.
- Cut puff pastry circles with lattice cutter or by hand making incisions even and between each line, using small paring knife.
- Season beef fillets and sear with oil in a frying pan.
- Spread some mushroom duxelle on top of beef, add a small slice of foie gras, and cover with a pastry circle.
- Place on a non-stick tray brushed with butter, a good distance between each other, and paint with egg yolk.
- Bake for 10-12 mins 210-220C Gas Mark 7.
- After 6 mins turn tray 180 degrees for even golden colour.
- When cooked, remove and leave to rest in a warm place for 10-15 mins. The beef will be more tender this way, will not ooze blood, and will retain its juices.

Presentation

- Serve with preferred vegetables such as baby carrots, new potatoes and spinach, plus a Madeira gravy*.

6

5 announcing Rolling Stones World
Tour in New York 2002

6 Bianca Jagger

For Mick Jagger, Elena recommends...

Beef Wellington with Vegetables and Madeira Gravy

...for unsurpassed stamina

Princess Diana

I had no idea that Diana, Princess of Wales was coming to L'Escargot when she turned up for dinner one night in a party of eight, with her detective who sat discreetly at a table nearby. She was charming and elegant, and we had a brief chat when I welcomed her. I remember that she chose fish.

A few people stared, of course, but not overtly. She was totally relaxed. I had a sudden shiver of unease when one of my other customers, a man sitting at another table, suddenly said to me: "Oh, I see you've got class in here today." I had seen him in the restaurant before, but never really got to know him. Now he was being sarcastic. Why, I have no idea, but I didn't reply or rise to the bait.

Next day the phone started ringing. It was the gossip columnists, all of them asking the same question: "Is it right that Diana was crying last night? What was going on? We had a call that she was in tears."

I was taken aback, but recovered swiftly. "I never saw anything like that," I told them "If she had any tears it must have been because she was laughing!" But it was no use. The day after, the papers were full of it. *Diana Upset in Celebrity Restaurant*, that kind of thing. But none of it was true. She had certainly been enjoying herself, and she may have dabbed her eyes with her napkin because she was laughing so much. They were the only tears she shed that night.

I was terribly upset. That's the kind of publicity you *don't* need. I had a friend I valued very much – Sir William Heseltine, the Queen's principal private secretary. And I thought: he'll think it was me who tipped the papers off.

I rang Buckingham Palace, and they put me through to him in Balmoral. I felt I had to apologise for the media mentioning that Princess Diana was crying in my restaurant. Bill said: "Don't worry, Elena. We all know you wouldn't do such a thing." I felt slightly better after that.

But it shows how stories can end up the wrong way – and it sticks. I'm sure the sarcastic customer tipped off the paper – because after that I never saw him again.

1 with Prince Harry in Majorca 1987

2 at the Dior 50th Anniversary, New York 1996

3 touring Egypt in 1992

1 3

Ingredients – serves 4

1kg whole tuna loin
300g Puy black lentils
1 lemon
4 roasted red peppers
1 bunch coriander
4 vine tomatoes
1 tspn curry powder
1 tspn fish sauce (Squid brand)
200g Maris Piper potatoes

4 at the Serpentine Gallery, Hyde Park, London, 1994

5 with Jemima Khan in Pakistan 1996

5

Method

- Place the black lentils in a saucepan, cover with water and cook for 25 mins until 'al dente'*.
- Place the cooked lentils in a bowl and add the following ingredients:
  roasted red pepper – chopped, red chilli – chopped, curry powder, vinaigrette* and chopped fresh coriander.
- Meanwhile, blanch the potatoes cut into cubes and fry for 10 mins.
- Cut the tuna into four slices and cook in a grill pan oiled with a little vegetable oil.
- Place over a hot ring and grill for 50 seconds each side for medium rare.

For Princess Diana, Elena recommends...

Rare Grilled Tuna with Spicy Puy Lentils and Greek Yoghurt

...unique in style and taste

Presentation

- Place the warm lentil mix in the centre of a hot main course dish and put some blanched potatoes around the plate.
- Add spoons of Greek yoghurt* between the potatoes.
- Cut the tuna slice in three and place carefully on top of the lentils.
- Garnish with a single chervil leaf.

Sir Sean Connery was one of the star guests at the party to dedicate our largest private dining room to British Winners of the Oscars. It was held in 1996 to celebrate the centenary of L'Etoile – and what a night it was! The street was knee-deep in photographers, and we had some great names to celebrate the occasion.

One reason the likes of Richard Attenborough, John Mills, Jeremy Irons and Ben Kingsley were there was to meet Oscar winners less known to the public, but who were gods in their own right to these actors. I'm talking about cinematographic "greats" like Freddie Young, Jack Cardiff and Billy Williams, along with the director John Schlesinger and the lyricist Don Black. We have all their photographs on the walls, and more than fifty other framed Oscar winners.

I've known Sean for years, before he first starred as James Bond in *Dr No* and became an international mega-star. On this wonderful night he was with his wife Micheline, a petite, flame-headed French painter he married secretly in Marrakesh during the filming of *The Man who would be King*. After the opening ceremony they sat down to dinner with Jeremy Irons and Ben Kingsley at their table. Some time before midnight Sean asked me to call him a taxi, as he had to get back to his hotel to take a call from Hollywood.

I did so, but as he got up from the table a girl suddenly appeared who was dressed very sexily, and literally entwined herself round him. She shamelessly linked her arm through his and smiled up at him with the kind of look Delilah must have given Samson. Now Sean, of course, has had women chasing him all his life, particularly after Bond.

My husband Aldo was by the exit, and Sean caught his eye. Aldo saw the girl, and lifted up one arm, meaning: "Give her the elbow!" She had 'hooker' written all over her! Without making a scene I'd tried to prise the girl off him, but she clung on like a limpet.

I said to Micheline: "I'm ever so sorry, I couldn't get her off." Micheline smiled, and said quietly: "Don't worry, my dear. I'm quite used to it!"

Now that lady has class. Sean and Micheline have now been married more than thirty years and I think she realises she need have no worries in that quarter!

Sean Connery

1 in 'Goldfinger' 1964

2 in 'The Untouchables' 1987

3 in 'The Hunt for Red October' 1990

4 with Harrison Ford in 'Indiana Jones and the Last Crusade' 1989

4

Ingredients – serves 4

4 x 250g Ribeye steaks
200g spinach
200g cep mushrooms
vegetable oil
pinch nutmeg
salt and pepper

Cep Sauce

100g field mushrooms
100g dried ceps – soaked
50g butter
3 shallots, sliced
2 cloves garlic, chopped
small bunch of thyme
150ml vermouth
250ml chicken stock*
250ml double cream

Method

Cep sauce*

- Sweat* shallots and garlic in a saucepan without colour in butter.
- Add field mushrooms and soaked Ceps and cook for 10 mins on a low heat.
- Add vermouth and reduce by half on a high heat.
- Add chicken stock* and reduced by ⅔.
- Add cream and cook for further 10 mins.
- Blend sauce in liquidiser and pass through a fine sieve.
- Season well.

Ribeye Steak

- Pan fry steak in vegetable oil as preferred, slice and serve.
- Toss spinach in a hot pan for 30 secs with a knob of butter.
- Add a pinch of nutmeg.
- Salt and pepper to season.

Presentation

- Garnish with freshly wilted spinach, a few sautéed fresh Ceps and Elena's chips*.
- Sautée cep mushrooms with knob of butter for 2 mins and season with salt and pepper.

5

6

5 with Daniela Bianchi in 'From Russia With Love' 1963

6 on holiday in Turkey 2005

Ribeye Steak with a Cep Sauce, Spinach and Elena's Chips

...it has to be beefsteak for Sean

Rod Stewart walked into L'Etoile with a tall and beautiful blonde on his arm. This one was the model Penny Lancaster, who stands 6ft 1 ins – a vital statistic which didn't surprise me. Rod's reputation with women is written into folk lore, particularly his penchant for tall blondes. The fact that he's close to 60 and Penny is almost 30 years younger makes not a scrap of difference to his magnetism.

As usual, we got chatting. I said to them: "I'm going to tell you a funny story – and I hope you're going to laugh at it. I've never told anyone this before."

Rod raised an eyebrow. I looked at the girl, and told her: "Don't worry about what I'm going to say, dear." She looked equally bemused.

I turned to Rod. "Many years ago you came to eat at Bianchi's, and you had a white suit on. I had no idea who you were, but I knew there were a lot of paparrazzi hanging around outside, which always meant a celebrity in the restaurant. Then it dawned on me: I didn't know your name, but I burst out: 'Oh, my goodness! I know where I've seen you before. In my son's bedroom! *It's you!*'"

Penny looked at Rod. Rod looked at Penny. They both shook their heads. Hastily I went on: "You looked quite stunned, and exclaimed: 'What? I've never been in your son's bedroom!'

"I told you: 'No, I don't mean *that!* It was a poster. It covered about half the wall!' As I say, at that time I had no idea who Rod Stewart was.

Rod, radiating Mr Cool, inquired: "How old is your son, Elena?"

"He's over fifty now."

"Me, too," said Rod. "That was my time, wasn't it!"

So, no scandal there. Rod gave a huge chortle – and so did Penny!

1 at the World Music Awards, Monte Carlo, 2001

2 in concert in Rio de Janiero, Brazil, 1985

3 at Bobby Moore Fund football charity match 2004

Rod Stewart

2

Ingredients – serves 2

2 fillets halibut approx
800g each
200g Maris Piper potatoes
5 leaves of basil
100g courgette
100g carrot
½ lemon
1 star anis
100g fresh spinach
½ bunch chervil
1 tspn salt
fish sauce*
50g tomato

Method

- Place the courgette and carrot in a small saucepan of water.
- Bring to the boil and cook for 4-5 mins until 'al dente'*
- Dice vegetables and refresh by soaking in ice-cold water.
- Use a bain marie to poach the halibut.
- Place half lemon, star anis, and 1 tsp of salt in sufficient water to cover the fish.
- Bring the bain marie to the boil on a high heat then simmer.
- Rinse the halibut fillets and place in the bain marie simmering for 8-10 mins.
- Clean spinach and toss in a hot pan with a knob of butter for 30-45 secs.

Presentation

- Reheat the vegetables, mash potatoes as normal and place in plastic piping bag.
- Pipe the plain mash on the centre of a main course size warm plate.
- Add spinach to top of the mash and place diced carrot and courgette around the plate.
- Replace the halibut fillets in the bain marie for 1 minute maximum then place on top of the spinach.
- Drizzle fish sauce* with chopped basil.
- Garnish with 'con casse'* tomato, lemon and a few leaves of chervil.

4 on 'Larry King Live TV' in America 2002

5 with Ronnie Wood at Olympic Torch concert

6 on German TV in 2002

For Rod Stewart, Elena recommends...

Poached Halibut with Mashed Potatoes, Carrots and Courgettes

...for his appetite for blondes

Robert de Niro

Robert de Niro walked into L'Etoile one cold winter's night for dinner. He was with Jonathan Pryce, an old friend. I had no idea he was coming, but of course I recognised him right away, even before I was introduced.

De Niro was polite and charming, and at first there were just the two of them. Then a stranger came to join them, an American. I took their order. The third man said "I don't want anything to eat." I said: Well, that's all right if you don't want to eat, but I think you should have a nice bowl of soup because it's freezing out there.

The three of them burst out laughing, and De Niro said: "You know what? She reminds me of Martin Scorcese's mother! It's the kind of thing she would do, ordering you about." Scorcese, of course, had directed him in several major films, including *Raging Bull* and *Taxi Driver*, and they were close friends. So his friend had the soup!

During the meal, one of my boys came over and asked for an autograph which is the one thing you don't do in my restaurant. De Niro signed his autograph, and when I heard I went over and apologised – in Italian! He spoke it beautifully, because his father was Italian, remember.

I said: "Scusa… *I'm sorry, I don't like my boys to ask for autographs. But now that you've given it to him. How can I tell my husband and son that a waiter got it and I didn't… they'd never forgive me!"* De Niro laughed and signed the restaurant card, to my husband Aldo and son Luis. Luis has it framed on his wall!

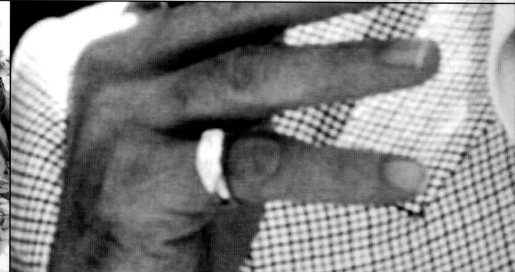

1 in 'Casino' 1995
2 with Ray Liotta, Paul Sorvino and Joe Pesci
  in 'Good Fellas' 1990
3 with Meryl Streep in 'Deer Hunter' 1978

For Robert de Niro, Elena recommends...

Confit of Welsh Lamb with Caper Sauce

...always a powerful performance

Ingredients – serves 4

1 boned shoulder of lamb
200g spinach
200g swede
40g coarse sea salt
10g castor sugar
1 onion
half head garlic
half bunch thyme
half bunch rosemary
15g anchovies
zest of 1 orange
caper sauce*
lamb stock*
50g fresh mint
25ml extra virgin olive oil and
25ml vegetable oil (mixed)

Method

- Blend the onion, zest of orange, sea salt, anchovies, rosemary and garlic to a paste.
- Rub paste over lamb and marinate for 24 hrs.
- Roll lamb, tie neatly, then wrap tightly in foil.
- Cook slowly for 4½ hrs at 160C Gas Mark 2-3 then remove.
- When cool (not cold) remove foil and wrap. tightly in clingfilm to form a good circular shape.
- Refrigerate for 24 hrs.
- Toss spinach with a knob of butter for 30 secs in a hot pan.

Presentation

- Cut lamb into circles one and a half inches thick.
- Reheat slowly in a well flavoured lamb stock.*
- Place on some spinach pressed into a cutter (pastry mould) or plain mashed potato if preferred as shown.
- Surround with caper sauce.*
- Garnish with cubes of swede and a little flat leafed parsely.

7 in 'Raging Bull' 1980

John Lennon & Yoko Ono

John Lennon and Yoko Ono were familiar faces at Bianchi's when they were first going out together. They had met at an art show at the Indica Gallery in London in 1966, and became an "item" soon after. I heard that John became intrigued with her because of one item at the exhibition: a framed piece of paper displayed on the ceiling. He climbed up a ladder with a magnifying glass to read whatever was on the paper, All it said was one word: "Yes". Well, that's one way to start a romance!

They always asked for Table 7, and it was immediately obvious to me how besotted John was with this strange Japanese lady who had an almost mystical air about her. Didn't they spend a week lying in bed in the Amsterdam Hilton declaring Flower Peace, Love Peace and even Hair Peace?

An extraordinary thing happened the first time they came to my restaurant. I handed the menus to them as I do with every customer – only to have Yoko snatch it out of John's hand, mull over it carefully herself, then order for both of them! This was long before they were married, in the early days.

John just sat there gazing at her, without saying a word. Whenever I passed their table it seemed they were sitting in silence – but quite happily. I would ask: "Is everything all right?" Meaning the food, of course. And it would be Yoko who smiled and said: "Yes, everything's fine."

They were totally engrossed in one another, more than any couple I can recall. Talk about a pair of love birds! I couldn't believe how intently he stared at her. He could have been in a trance. Yoko dominated the whole situation, always chose for both of them, and even paid the bill at the end. As for the food, they liked pasta, but mainly they would both have the same thing – gnocchi verdi, which is actually a dumpling.

1 the Beatles in 1967

2 filming Help at Cliveden in 1965

3 at a Yoko Ono art exhibition, Mayfair, London, 1968

3

4 Beatles promo film for Sergeant
Pepper fashions in 1968

5 at a rally in 1969

Method

- Clean spinach and blanch in boiling salted water for 10 secs.
- Drain, press dry and chop finely.
- Mash ricotta into a paste.
- Place spinach in pan with salt, pepper, nutmeg, butter and mashed ricotta.
- Stir over low flame for 5 mins.
- Remove and beat in eggs, grated Parmesan, flour and a plain mashed potato.
- Leave in fridge overnight.
- Spread pastry board with flour, roll into small croquettes (by hand).
- Drop carefully into pan of boiling water, slightly salted, leaving plenty of space between them.
- Gnocchi will rise to the surface after 3 mins, or when cooked.
- Remove and drain carefully in a colander.
- Slide into pre-heated oven at 180C Gas Mark 4 with 30g butter and grated parmesan cheese.
- Leave for 5 mins. before serving.

Ingredients – serves 4

125g ricotta fresh
cream cheese
50g butter
100g grated Parmesan
2 eggs
50g flour
250g cooked and
chopped spinach
salt and pepper
nutmeg
125g Maris Piper potatoes
4 vine tomatoes
1 bunch sage

WAR
IS
OVER!

Presentation

- Place gnocchi dumplings in centre of plate.
- Blanch the tomatoes for 30 secs to remove skin.
- Refresh in iced water and remove seeds.
- Cut into quarter 'flowers' and carefully place on top of each dumpling.
- Drizzle green chive sauce* round rim of plate for effect and finish with a few sage leaves.

For John Lennon & Yoko Ono, Elena recommends...

Gnocchi Verdi with Tomato and Green Chive Sauce

...their regular choice

Michael Palin

Michael Palin is something of a phenomenon. To judge by his frequent appearances on TV and the radio, you'd think he was a workaholic who never stops moving – whichever part of the world he finds himself in. It's true he's a live wire, but he never seems stressed out, and comes across to me as the eternal optimist. I think that shows in his great globe-trotting TV travel programmes.

We go back to the Bianchi's days when he would book a table for six or eight, and turn up with the entire *Monty Python* cast. You can imagine the mayhem that caused – with John Cleese, Graeme Garden, Terry Gilliam and the rest of the crew unwinding together, the table was in paroxysms of laughter from start to finish – the finish usually being in the early hours when I had to throw them all out!

While at L'Escargot my lasting memory is seeing a huge blow-up red dragon suddenly appearing on the staircase to the upstairs room where Michael was celebrating his birthday party for fifty or so guests. Looking closer, I spied the perspiring face of John Cleese manhandling the creature from below to give his old friend a surprise. It occurs to me now that Michael may have seen the real thing on his travels to some far-flung corner of the earth. I must ask him some time!

1 with John Cleese in 'Life of Brian' 1979

2 filming a documentary in Split, Croatia, 2006

3 with 'Monty Python' team Eric Idle, Terry Jones, John Cleese, Graham Chapman, Terry Gilliam in 1989

114

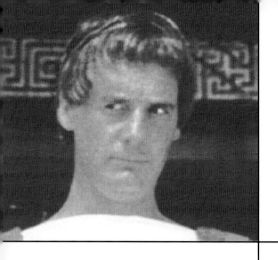

Salmon and Leek Fishcake with Chive Green Sauce, Elena's Chips and Mushy Peas

...they both travel well

Ingredients – to serve 4

500g salmon fillet (skin off)
100g Maris Piper potatoes
1 small leek
½ tblspn tomato ketchup
1 tblspn coarse grain mustard
200g Japonaise breadcrumbs
1 bunch dill

Bechamel Sauce
100g flour
100ml milk
50g of unsalted butter
pinch nutmeg,
salt and pepper

Method – Bechamel sauce
- Melt butter in pan.
- When bubbling, but before turning brown, add flour through wire sieve.
- Stir gently with a wooden spoon into a thick creamy substance.
- Add hot milk, stir vigorously.
- Season with salt, pepper and a little nutmeg.
- Add salmon juice retained from cooking.
- Sauce should be thick.

Method – fishcakes
- Sweat* finely chop leeks in butter.
- Place salmon in oven on a hot tray 200C Gas Mark 6 for 5-7 mins so it's still pink inside. Put into a bowl.
- Sweat finely chopped leeks in butter.
- Add to salmon then add 50g mashed potato.
- Add 2 tblspns bechamel sauce* and flavour with salt and pepper.
- Add 1 tblspn coarse grain mustard, ½ tblspn tomato ketchup, plus any juice from cooking salmon.
- Mix together in the container.
- Press it into symmetrical shapes (approx 4 ins wide) with a pastry cutter
- Place in freezer to set until firm (up to 2 hrs).
- Once firm, cover first in flour, next in beaten egg, finally in breadcrumbs blended with dill to obtain an attractive green colour.
- Deep or shallow fry for 2 mins to retain moisture and flavour.
- Then cook in oven for 8 mins to heat all the way through at 180C Gas Mark 4.

Presentation
- Serve with a chive green sauce*, and a little salad on top of the fishcake.
- Final touch add famous Elena's chips* and mushy peas*

4 opening the new glasshouse at Kew Gardens, London, 2006

5 with John Cleese on set of 'A Fish Called Wanda' 1988

Richard Attenborough

Among the many offices he holds, Lord Attenborough is chairman of the Actors' Charitable Trust and Denville Hall, their retirement home at Denham, Bucks.. L'Etoile supports this worthwhile charity – with our show-business history it's a natural marriage – and when you use our private dining room, dedicated to British Oscar Winners, for a private function a proportion of the fee goes to the home.

Just as that other titled icon Sir John Mills was known as Johnny, Lord A. hates formality and would rather be called Dickie than "my lord". He is a wonderfully avuncular figure, with his patriarchal white beard (didn't he once play Father Christmas?). But that's the only sign of the passing years. "Dickie" is as young as springtime, whatever the season, and he lightens up my restaurant every time he sets foot in it – which I'm glad to say is quite often.

Over the years I've discovered his secret. It's very simple: he makes everyone he meets feel special. That's his way. He's very touchy-feely – it's hugs and embraces all round, but believe me, it's all genuine, unlike the horrid "moi-moi air-kissing" that now seems to be part of the celebrity culture.

I actually think there's something else about him. With a massive career behind him, Dickie still enjoys life. And if that rubs off, who's complaining?

1 in 'The Great Escape' 1963

2 with Peter Sellers in 'Only Two Can Play' 1962

3 receiving Oscars in 1983 for 'Gandhi' with Best Actor Ben Kingsley and Meryl Streep

4 directing Anthony Hopkins and Debra Winger in 'Shadowlands' 1993

Method

- Cut and shape carrot, courgette and turnip.
- Place in a large saucepan of water, bring to the boil and cook for 4-5 mins until 'al dente'*.
- Refresh vegetables in a bowl of iced water.
- Care is needed in cooking veal kidneys as they can quickly overcook Heat a medium sized non stick pan with a little extra virgin olive oil.
- Place kidneys in the pan and seal the skin into a brown colour cooking for 4-5 mins on a medium heat.

Presentation

- Reheat vegetables and mix with 3 tblspns of cream.
- Place creamed vegetables on a flat plate.
- Add the cooked kidneys to the top of the vegetables, and drizzle the mustard sauce*.
- Garnish with chervil leaves.

Ingredients – serves 2

800g of raw veal kidneys
½ of a 100g turnip
½ of a 100g carrot
½ of a 100g courgette
100ml double cream
1 bunch chervil
mustard sauce*

5 With Jeff Goldblum, Laura Dern and Sam Neill in Jurassic Park 1993

6 With wife Sheila Sim on the set of 'Dancing With Crime' 1947

For Richard Attenborough, Elena recommends...

Veal Kidneys with Creamed Vegetables and Mustard Sauce

...a rare talent indeed

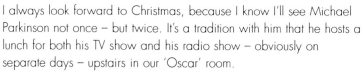

Michael Parkinson

I always look forward to Christmas, because I know I'll see Michael Parkinson not once – but twice. It's a tradition with him that he hosts a lunch for both his TV show and his radio show – obviously on separate days – upstairs in our 'Oscar' room.

I never know quite how many guests will be there until Mike calls me at the last moment to confirm numbers. It's a generous gesture, and he pays for everything out of his own pocket rather than the company's, but when I told him so recently he just shrugged and said: "Elena, it's the least I can do. These are the people who put the programmes together, and I couldn't do it without them. It's just a small thank-you to show my appreciation." Mike always insists I tell the story about his old friend the presenter the late Bill Grundy, who was another regular at L'Escargot and L'Etoile. His dinner parties were legendary, not just for the amount of wine consumed but for the fact that they'd go on into the early hours, despite my efforts to get everyone into taxis and see them off the premises. I always managed to stop myself from saying: "Don't you lot have homes to go to?" – though sometimes it was a close thing.

The story Mike loves is how Bill was well and truly in his cups one night, and insisted on a bottle of whisky to take home with him. "I'm sorry," I said. "We're all locked up, and the bar is closed." "Can't you take that bottle off the wall?" he said, somewhat indistinctly, gesturing at the upside-down bottles behind the bar. "I can't do that!" I said, horrified at the idea. "Everything has to be accounted for."

It was true – it would be more than my job was worth. "Please, Elena," he pleaded. "You must have a bottle somewhere."

To my shame, I weakened. "All right, I'll get you one from the store room." I had the key, and climbed two flights to unlock it, reappearing with a bottle of the amber liquid. "Elena, you're an angel," cried the swaying figure. He grabbed the bottle, tucked it under his jacket, and headed for the door – when *CRASH!* The bottle slipped from his coat and shattered into pieces – inside the restaurant. Which meant I had to clear up the mess. "Out! *OUT!*" This time Bill went without a murmur. And for some reason Parky finds it hilarious to this day.

2

3

1 with Sharon Osbourne 'Royal Variety Performance' 2005

2 at the British Book Awards 2002

3 with Paul McCartney – 'Parkinson' 2005

★

ELENA'S

L'Etoile

For Michael Parkinson, Elena recommends...

Roast Guinea Fowl with Sage and Onion Stuffing and Pommes Fondant

...he's game for almost anything

Ingredients – serves 4

4 guinea fowl breasts
1 bunch of sage
½ packet of butter
1 whole onion finely chopped
2 cloves garlic
225g coarse white breadcrumbs
200g baby carrots

Method

Stuffing

- Sweat* onions and garlic in the half packet of butter until they are soft and translucent.
- Chop finely half a bunch of sage, add bread crumbs and place everything in a bowl.
- Allow to cool, then by hand mould into small sausage shapes. Lift guinea fowl skin slightly off the breast at the back by the wing bone, and insert stuffing under the skin.

Guinea fowl breasts

- Roast the breasts (5-10 mins at 200C Gas Mark 6).
- Always seal breast flesh side down to retain shape of the bird.
- Turn and roast on skin side to get a nice colour.
- Remove from oven and allow to rest for 5 mins.

Presentation

- Serve with Maris Piper pommes fondant*. (small round potatoes cooked in chicken stock with butter).
- Use wings of the guinea fowl to make a sauce (as brown sauce)*.
- Serve with preferred vegetables eg baby carrots or green beans.

4 with Jamie Foxx – 'Parkinson' 2006

5 with Jane Fonda – 'Parkinson' 2006

6 with Madonna – 'Parkinson' 2005

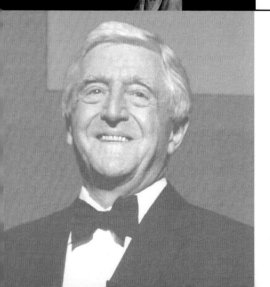

Ella Fitzgerald

At Bianchi's a big, swarthy-looking man came in every night and sat upstairs by himself at the same table by the window, watching the street below. Every night. Always the same table. He was American, and I began to wonder if anyone was after him – like maybe the Mafia. Quite often he would be halfway through his meal when he would suddenly get up, throw some money on the table, and disappear out into the night.

The first few times I didn't say anything. But after a week of this behaviour I finally spoke up. "Excuse my asking, but is someone looking for you? You never finish your meal." That's me, straight and to the point.

He laughed and replied: "No, it's not like that at all. Ella Fitzgerald is appearing at Ronnie Scott's, and I'm her road manager." He gestured across the street. "I have

to go out there when Ella arrives and see her safely into her dressing-room."

The following night was different. He suddenly reappeared, hurrying back to ask if I could get a dish of pasta – *fettucini a la crema* ready for ten-thirty on the dot. No problem. But then he added: "It's for Ella. And I want you to take it across. I might drop it!"

Anything to oblige. I walked out across the street with a tray and a cloth over it, and was ushered inside like a VIP past the waiting queue. And that's how I ended up in Ella Fitzgerald's dressing-room, seeing her show, and becoming a personal friend of that extraordinary woman for years to come.

She must have liked the pasta, too, because she ordered it every time she came into my restaurants.

ELENA'S
L'Etoile

Ingredients – to serve 4

200g raw linguini
200g broad beans (skin off)
50g Parmesan
zest of 1 lemon
1 tblspn chopped basil
1 tblspn chopped parsley
1 tblspn chopped chives
2 tblspns crème fraiche

Method

- First cook the pasta 'al dente'*.
- Then allow to cool very quickly in iced water.
- Drain, then run some olive oil through it and store in fridge until required.
- Blanch broad beans in well salted water.
- Again cool quickly in iced water.
- Once cool, pop out of skins and keep in fridge until needed.

To serve – have pot of boiling water ready

- Plunge pasta and broad beans into the water in a basket.
- In a separate pan put in the crème fraiche – reduce a little.
- Add a good pinch of Parmesan.
- Drain pasta and beans, add the cream, season, add pinch of lemon zest and the herbs.
- Mix well, baste correct seasoning and serve.

For Ella Fitzgerald, Elena recommends...

Linguini Elena

...always pasta for Ella

Presentation
- Place into warm bowls.
- Sprinkle some Parmesan and a little lemon zest on top to finish.

Melvyn Bragg

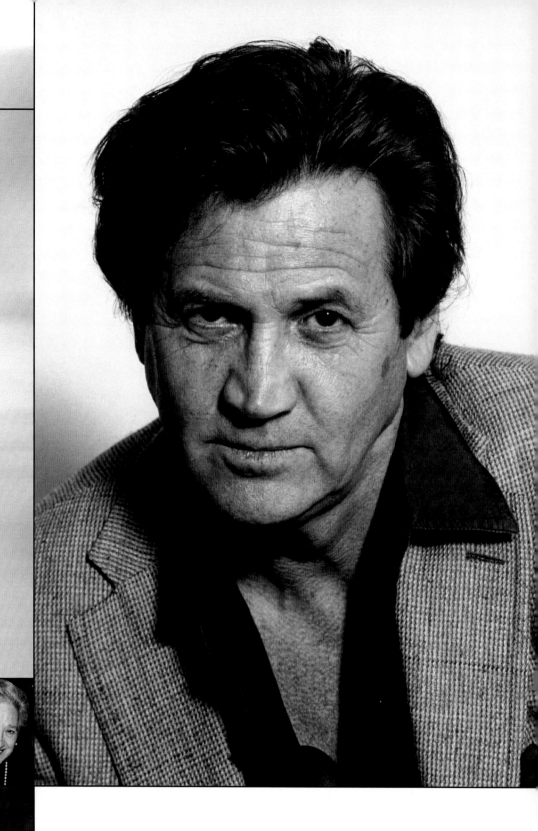

Melvyn – or Lord Bragg of Wigton, named after his home town in Cumbria – has eaten as often as three times a week in my restaurants. At L'Escargot he always had Table 8 by the wall, because, as he said: "You were pretty well out of the way there and can't be easily spotted." Melvyn values his privacy, despite being an instantly recognisable face with all his TV appearances.

At L'Etoile I have a photo of him on the wall holding a tray while celebrating a private party in one of the rooms upstairs. It contains, of all things, a plate of black puddings which you may think odd for the man who was once described by *Cosmopolitan* magazine as "the thinking woman's crumpet". Who am I to question black pudding or crumpet?

Because of the long-running *South Bank Show*, people tend to forget that Melvyn is a prolific writer. Apart from novels, he wrote the scripts of such films as Ken Russell's *The Music Lovers*, as well as *Jesus Christ, Superstar* and *Isadora*. He comes in for business lunches or with his wife Cate Haste, herself a writer and TV producer – and I have to check the date when I see him arrive.

If it's the first week of the month, that means no wine for Melvyn – for years he has disciplined himself to drink nothing stronger than sparkling water for one week out of four. "You could say I have three weeks to drink and one to dry out," he explained to me. Full marks for will power – and since Melvyn fancies fish I know he'll probably have a Pouilly Fumé white wine. Depending on the date, of course.

Ingredients – serves 4

4 x 160g slices calves liver
600g Maris Piper potatoes
1 bunch home-dried sage
80g Japonaise breadcrumbs
200g spinach
1 tblspn coarse grain mustard
knob of butter

Method

- Blend Japonaise breadcrumbs and sage together in food mixer to form a rough crumble and set aside.
- Season each side of calves liver slices and pass through the sage crumb.
- Mash potatoes as normal adding coarse grain mustard and taste frequently to achieve desired flavour.
- Pan fry liver as preferred in mix of 50% butter and 50% extra virgin olive oil.
- Toss spinach with knob of butter for 30 secs in a hot pan.

Presentation

- Serve liver with mash, spinach and brown sauce gravy*.

For Melvyn Bragg, Elena recommends...

Calves Liver in a Sage Crust with Mustard Mash

...his first choice for lunch

David Jason

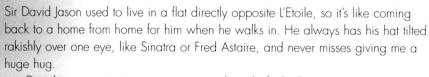

Sir David Jason used to live in a flat directly opposite L'Etoile, so it's like coming back to a home from home for him when he walks in. He always has his hat tilted rakishly over one eye, like Sinatra or Fred Astaire, and never misses giving me a huge hug.

David is very outgoing, very warm and touchy-feely. For some reason, whenever I see him that classic TV scene jumps into my mind where he has his arm

on the bar and falls over. We go back a long way – all the way to Bianchi's, and the days of *Open All Hours*, *Only Fools and Horses* and *Darling Buds of May*.

It has been a joy to watch him mature into a great actor. Now, when I see him as Frost with that severity you never saw in him in his younger roles, I hardly think it's the same man.

But that's the mark of a good actor, isn't it – constantly being able to surprise you.

1 with Nicholas Lyndhurst filming
'Only Fools and Horses', Bristol,
1996

2 on set in 'Darling Buds of May'
1992

3 at Royal International Air Tattoo
RAF Fairford 2004

For David Jason, Elena recommends...

Saddle of Lamb with New Potatoes, Baby Carrots and Rosemary Jus

... 'perfeck' in every way

Method

- Cook 200g of new potatoes in boiling water for 10-12 mins.
- Roll the puff pastry into small pieces 8cm square.
- Make sure the rolled pastry is even in size and shape
- Meanwhile, seal the fillets of saddle of lamb in a hot pan.
- Cut lamb into 2 fillets and cover with the puff pastry rolled earlier.
- Put the covered lamb fillets in fridge to chill.

Ingredients – serves 2

1 large fillet saddle of lamb
200g new potatoes
1 bunch baby carrots
1 bunch rosemary
200g fresh spinach
50g packet of puff pastry
1 egg yolk
rosemary jus sauce*

Presentation

- Rub a little butter on a non stick tray.
- Place the two fillets of saddle lamb on the tray and brush the pastry cover with 1 egg yolk.
- Cook in oven for 4-6 mins at 220C Gas Mark 7.
- This will cook to perfection with the lamb medium rare inside and the puff pastry golden on the outside.
- Meanwhile toss the fresh spinach in a hot pan with a knob of butter for 30-45 secs and place on the centre of a warm plate.
- Warm the cooked new potatoes and set around the spinach.
- Blanch the baby carrots in boiling water for 30 secs.
- Cut each fillet of lamb in half and place on the spinach.
- Drizzle rosemary jus sauce* on to the plate.
- Garnish with fresh rosemary and the baby carrots.

4

5

4 filming 'Micawber' in 2000

5 at National Television Awards, London, 2003

6 at Daily Mirror 'Pride of Britain Awards', London 2004

6

John Hurt

John is one of my favourites. He has been a regular at all my restaurants, and quite often I sit down and have a chat after he has finished eating. Some time ago he was in for dinner, and as usual I said to him: "What are you up to, John – anything interesting?"

He replied: "I'm not sure. They've asked me to do the Alan Clark diaries, and I'm still thinking about it." I burst out: "Oh, you've got to! You're a natural for it. You and all those ladies. That role is tailor-made for you – it'll be type-casting!" He took it, of course. He's a brilliant actor, and the series was brilliant too.

Actually it was the second time I stuck my oar into a career move for John. In 1988 he was offered the crucial role of osteopath Stephen Ward in *Scandal*, the film about the Christine Keeler affair that cost John Profumo his Government job. He had been in Paris, he recalled, when Profumo resigned. "The French papers took the view that he was being dismissed for having a mistress, whereas in France a Minister would be dismissed for not having a mistress," he joked.

In fact he didn't want to do it, and one night we had a ferocious argument. John was in a mood, and he said: "I've had enough, Elena. I'm fed up, I'm going to chuck the whole thing in." I was horrified. "You can't do that!" I cried. "You're an actor. You're wonderful. Besides, what else would you do?"

He must have thought about it, because the next night I saw him at a function at the Café Royal, and there he was on the stairs. He spotted me, and shouted down: "I'm going to do it!" And he did, playing a man who, in his own words "wasn't a saint, but had committed no crime other than snobbery and social climbing." Naturally, John was brilliant again!

1 'Heroes' at Wyndham's Theatre, London, 2005

2 Krapp's Last Tape – Barbican, London, 2006-

3 with Danny Huston in 'The Proposition' 2006

4 '1984' the film, in 1984

5 with Claire Hope Ashley in 'Shooting Dogs' 2005

4

5

ELENA'S L'Étoile

For John Hurt, Elena recommends...

Honey and Black Pepper Roasted Duck Breast with Garlic, French Beans and Potato Rosti

...full of delicious flavour

Ingredients – serves 4

4 x 200g female duck breasts
150ml double cream
1 tblspn honey
50g cracked black pepper
250g French beans
1 head garlic
400g Maris Piper potatoes
100ml milk
1 bunch thyme
salt

6 in Scandal 1989

Method

Garlic Cream
- Break garlic into cloves, chop and cook in saucepan of milk on low heat for 5 mins and drain.
- Bring double cream to boil and add cooked garlic.
- Take off heat, leave for 2 mins, then blend or mash into a fine purée.

Potato Rosti
- Heat 4 small non-stick blini pans.
- Shred and salt potatoes.
- Leave for 10 mins until soft, then squeeze out excess moisture.
- Mix in 1 tblspn of calcified butter and small pinch of thyme leaves.
- Push this mixture into lightly oiled pans with the back of a spoon.
- Cook on medium heat.
- When mix starts to colour, add a small knob of butter, turn and repeat for a golden colour on both sides.

French Beans
- Blanch in well salted water and cook until just past 'al dente'* but not too soft.
- Keep tasting, then plunge into iced water.
- Retain until needed.

Duck Breast
- Season duck breasts well with salt (they should be well trimmed and scored on top).
- Place in hot pan, skin side down.
- Tip away any resulting fat, then place in hot oven at 200C Gas Mark 6 for 5 mins still on the skin side.
- When cooked remove from oven.
- Brush with honey which has been acidulated with lemon juice, then press into cracked black pepper.
- Cook for 1 more min in a medium-hot pan, then leave to rest in a warm place for 10 mins.

Presentation

- Warm rosti, place in middle of plate.
- Reheat French beans, drain then place in pan with a little butter and 1tblspn of garlic cream.
- Season to taste and place on top of potato.
- Slice duck breast and fan around the plate.

141

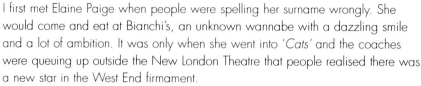

Elaine Paige

I first met Elaine Paige when people were spelling her surname wrongly. She would come and eat at Bianchi's, an unknown wannabe with a dazzling smile and a lot of ambition. It was only when she went into 'Cats' and the coaches were queuing up outside the New London Theatre that people realised there was a new star in the West End firmament.

Then she won the starring role in *Evita*, and the world really sat up and took notice. Elaine would be joined at the table by Andrew Lloyd Webber and Tim Rice, and they became a regular threesome as *Evita* took shape. I was aware that something big was going on, but I had no idea just *how* big it would turn out to be.

Andrew was like the White Rabbit, always in a hurry. A glance at the menu, and he ordered very quickly. Then he was gone. The night of the world premiere of *Evita*, they brought Elaine in to the restaurant in the afternoon for a one-to-one interview with a national daily paper. It struck me as odd, because the girl obviously had a lot more on her mind than telling some stranger all about her life. I was right. Poor Elaine was a bag of nerves.

It didn't help that outside the theatre in Old Compton Street there were noisy protests going on. People were parading with banners and shouting slogans, more concerned that Elaine might be making a political statement than trying to do her bit in a big stage musical. Elaine didn't want to know – but she couldn't help being dragged into it. The protesters complained that she was portraying Eva Peron as a goddess rather than an ambitious model who seduced a president – even though, as Elaine told me, once you saw the play you knew very well it was telling you what she was really like.

She came in to be interviewed wearing a white leather suit, and was shaking like a jelly. There were only a few hours to go before curtain up. I took her aside to a corner table, sat her down, and told her quietly: "Listen, Elaine. You're going to be all right, girl. Don't worry about the protesters. You've got a wonderful night ahead of you, one you'll remember all your life. Be proud that you've been chosen to do it. Get up there! This is what you're good at. You can do it."

And she did. She never forgot it, and we've been friends ever since. She got through that interview, and went out and wowed 'em!

Now she says: "Every time I think of you, Elena, I think of my mother." And I tell her: "I'm a second mother to a lot of people! But you're special." The truth is, of course, they all are.

2

1 opening night of 'The Misanthrope',
  Piccadilly Theatre, London 1998

2 in 'Chess' with Murray Head,
  Siobhan McCarthy and Tommy
  Korberg 1986

3 at a charity hat auction at
  Shakespeare's Globe. London, 2002

4 with Andrew Lloyd Webber
  launching 'Sunset Boulevard' in New
  York 1997

3

4

5 in 'Sunset Boulevard' New York 1997

6 at the Evening Standard Theatre
  Awards, Savoy Hotel, London 2003

Method

Salmon Potato Crust

- Heat oil to 120C and blanch shredded potatoes for 4-5 mins.
- Drain, cool, then mix in egg yolk and thyme leaves.
- Take some waxed parchment paper and press/spread potatoes evenly and not too firmly.
- Dust Salmon with flour to one side and press this side on to the potato.
- Cover salmon and place in the fridge.
- After 1 hour remove from fridge and cut around each piece of salmon.
- Turn over and leave waxed paper on until required.

Spinach

- Take a hot pan with a knob of butter.
- Toss spinach for 30 secs.
- Add a pinch of nutmeg.
- Salt and pepper to season.
- As an alternative, try this dish with Choucroute* (Sauerkraut) in place of spinach.

Ingredients – serves 4

4 x 180g pieces of salmon
300g fresh spinach
200g finely shredded Maris Piper potatoes
1 egg yolk with a few thyme leaves
pinch of nutmeg
salt and pepper

6

Presentation

- Cook salmon, potato side down, in a non-stick frying pan until golden and crispy.
- Turn and finish slowly for 3-4mins, adding a good knob of butter.
- Place spinach in the middle of the plate and position salmon on top.
- Finally, whisk a few knobs of butter, plus a sprinkle of thyme leaves and spin this around the plate to add flavours. If using choucroute, add some of the jus.
- Surround with green chive sauce*.

Roast Salmon Potato Crust with Spinach

...they share a magical versatility

Christopher Lee

At L'Etoile, every table is a celebrity table – when you walk in, you never know who you're going to find sitting where. But as with most restaurants, regulars always have their "own table" where they feel most comfortable. We have two window areas, with a table in each that seat four people. Otherwise, one particular favourite for celebs. is the first table on the right, just past a partition leading to the 'Oscar' room upstairs, where they can sit and see most of the restaurant without being noticed.

Christopher Lee was seated here on his first visit – and we got on famously after I introduced myself, welcomed him, and found we had something in common apart from a liking for good food...the Italian language. Christopher has an Italian ancestry with his family name traced to Count Carandini in 1184. Part of his imposing presence is his aristocratic bearing, and not just because he stands close to six-foot-four. His life story is amazing – as a teenager he even witnessed the last public execution by

2

guillotine in Paris. But our conversation was on less grisly lines, and somehow got around to singing.

"I always had a secret wish to be an opera singer," he confided. "I even trained for it, and once auditioned for a Noel Coward musical of *Lady Windermere's Fan*. At the end Noel said: 'You have a voice with a baritone quality.'

That was a nice compliment – but I still didn't get the role. So I decided to take the acting route instead."

The Royal Opera House's loss, the cinema's gain. Christopher has made so many films that I suspect he has lost count of them all. But it's somewhere close to 300, and very few show him baring his fangs as the screen's most famous Count Dracula.

"Well, I can promise you one thing," I assured him. "At least tonight you won't have to sing for your supper!"

1 in 'Man With the Golden Gun' 1974

2 with Barbara Shelly in 'Dracula, Prince of Darkness' 1966

147

Ingredients – serves 4

4 x 200g of lemon sole fillets
1kg Maris Piper potatoes
2 eggs
50g flour
200g spinach
2 tspn caper berries
100ml double cream
1 pinch saffron
pinch nutmeg
Maldon sea salt
Breadcrumbs mixture
100g Japonaise breadcrumbs
100g Parmesan
zest of 2 lemons

3 in 'The Wicker Man' 1973

Method
- Ask fishmonger to fillet and skin the sole and cut into finger size pieces.
- Breadcrumb the sole first in flour, then egg and finally, the breadcrumb mixture.
- Shallow or deep fry sole and drain. (Note: sole cooks very quickly!).
- Season with lemon salt made by mixing lemon zest into Maldon sea salt.

Saffron Mash
- Add saffron to the cream. Bring to the boil and leave on side for 15mins before straining. The resulting liquid will be very yellow and strong.

For Christopher Lee, Elena recommends...

Crispy Lemon Sole Fillets with Parmesan Crust, Saffron Mash and Caper Berries

...sinks his teeth into every role

- Make mash as normal, add one tblspn of saffron cream plus butter, salt, pepper and nutmeg.
- Result should be a nice yellow mash. If not dark enough, or needs more saffron flavour, add more cream to colour and taste.

Presentation
- Place mash on plate with some wilted spinach, position sole on top.
- Melt 50g butter in a pan until it froths.
- Add caper berries and parsley and spoon around the sole.

Albert Finney

Always expect the unexpected. That's one of my mottos, and it came in useful the night Albert Finney had booked a table for four for dinner at L'Escargot at ten-thirty. It was late, but he wanted to come on from a play in which he was starring.

People started arriving, all of them saying: "We're with Albert Finney", and in the end there were thirteen of them milling about. I thought: *How on earth am I going to handle this lot?* Somehow I was able to push a few empty tables together and fit them all in. The chef was about to pack up and go home. I rang down to the kitchen, and told him: "Listen, I'm not going to give them a menu – just send up fourteen dishes, whatever you've got to hand."

1 in 'Big Fish' 2003

2 in 'The Dresser'

3 in 'Murder on the Orient Express'
   1974

4 in 'Shoot the Moon' 1982

Finney came in last. I scolded him:" Albert, you told me four! You've given me fourteen!" He said: "What can I do?" I said: "You'll get what the chef sends up – all right?"

He said: "Don't worry, Elena. When mother puts food in front of us, we have to eat what she gives us. Go on, mother, give us what you like!"

The plates started coming up, and there I stood shouting out: "Who wants chicken? Who wants lamb?"

Albert announced: "Isn't it great, everyone? We don't have to worry about a menu. Mother's doing it for us." It worked a treat, and they all went away happy – some time in the early hours.

5

Ingredients – serves 4

500g bunch of asparagus
250g fresh ceps
1kg of Maris Piper potatoes
4 x 150g fillets of sea bass,
scaled and pin boned (ask your
fishmonger to do this)
and scored
250ml of cep sauce*
white truffle oil
50g butter
50g broad beans (skin off)

Method

- Snap bottoms of asparagus off where the green meets the white. Part and peel away from the delicate tip.
- Blanch in boiling salted water for 2 mins, then refresh in iced water. Cut in half lengthways, and half again the opposite way.
- Blanch broad beans in well salted water.
- Slice ceps and pan fry in butter until golden in colour.
- Season bass skin well and fry in a non-stick pan, skin side down, on a medium heat for 4 mins, then add a good knob of butter.
- Cook for a further 2 mins, then turn over and take the pan off the heat.
- Make potato mash as normal, but add a little white truffle oil and a good amount of butter to make a velvety consistency.

6

5 with Julia Roberts in 'Erin Brockovich' 2000

6 with Jessica Lange in 'Big Fish' 2003

For Albert Finney, Elena recommends...

Roast Sea Bass with Ceps, Asparagus and Truffle Potatoes

...hidden depths

Presentation

- Position mash in the middle of the plate with three pieces of asparagus and some sliced ceps and broad beans around the outside.
- Drizzle on some cep sauce* that has had one knob of butter whisked into it.

Ralph Fiennes

Ralph Fiennes had a wary look about him when he first stepped into L'Etoile. He is gloriously good looking, intense, intelligent, with huge sex appeal – and a look that sends out the message: *I want to be alone!* Or is it just me saying that?

All I know is that when I first set eyes on him I could almost read his thoughts. *"Are they going to fuss over me?"* It was the last thing he wanted. He just seems very shy – though he does sometimes take the window seat which can be seen from the street. I get a sixth sense about these things, which comes from experience. I felt it was important to keep that little bit of distance to make him feel comfortable – without ignoring him altogether, of course!

Ralph is a tremendous actor, and has done some marvellous work – from *Hamlet* on stage to films like *Schindler's List* and *The English Patient.* In the flesh he has this aura about him that gives rise to descriptions like "brooding" and even "Byronic".

But after a couple of visits he warmed up, and became quite cheery. As far as I was concerned, I was determined not to be put off, and said to him outright: "I want you up on my wall!" A few days later a signed picture came through the post – and it's hanging up there now.

1 The Constant Gardener 2005

2 Wuthering Heights 1992

3 Maid in Manhatten 2002

4 With Francesca Annis in Hamlet 1995

5 The Constant Gardener 2005

6 The Constant Gardener Trust Party for Africa,
Soho Hotel, London 2006

6

Ingredients – serves 2
2 x 300g cod fillets – (ask fishmonger for filleted and boned cod)
300g new potatoes
200ml double cream
200ml (homogenised) milk
200g cauliflower
100g spinach
2 pinches ground nutmeg
1 large vine tomato
1 lime
green chive sauce*

Method
- Prepare vegetables first.
- Boil new potatoes for 10-15 mins.
- Place chopped cauliflower in a mix of the milk and cream in a non stick saucepan adding 2 pinches of nutmeg.
- Bring to the boil and simmer for 10 mins to create a purée.
- Meanwhile blanch vine tomato for 10 secs in boiling water.
- Remove skin and shape or dice into cubes (con-casse*).
- Cut lime into thin slices.
- Use a bain marie to poach the cod.
- Bring to the boil enough water to cover the fillets adding half the sliced lime, the star anis and a pinch of salt.
- Add the cod fillets and simmer for 8-10 mins.

5

Presentation
- When cooked, the cod should be firm.
- Place some cauliflower purée on in the centre of a warm flat plate.
- Toss spinach in a hot pan with a knob of butter for 30 secs.
- Add spinach on top of the purée.
- Carefully position the cod fillets on top.
- Place new potatoes around the outside of the plate.
- Garnish with tomato con-casse* and slice of lime to add colou
- Pour the creamy green chive sauce* on to the plate.

Fillet of Poached Cod with New Potatoes, Spinach and Green Chive Sauce

...precision with a passion

2

3

Terence Stamp

We go back a long way, Terence Stamp and I. All the way back to the Bianchi days when he was part of the young tribe of actors who would come charging in for a late night (into early morning) meal at the end of their shows, mainly in Shaftesbury Avenue theatres. They were hungry, on a high, and the liveliest bunch you could wish for to make a restaurant sparkle. Terry had the most amazing eyes, huge and hypnotic. He still does.

In those days in the swinging sixties he was sharing a flat with his mate Michael Caine in Pimlico, and seemed to have a different girl on his arm every time he waltzed in. He still has that sex appeal, though he seems more serious now, and when

he comes in to L'Etoile it's a joy to reminisce about the "good old days". Because they really were good.

But next time Terry walks in, I have a little surprise for him. His picture hangs in the back room in pride of place where it can been seen all the way down the restaurant from the front entrance. But recently I spotted a small photograph that had been stuck casually in the bottom of the frame. It was a picture of another man, and when I turned it over, the person (I presume) had written in hand-writing: *I'm his brother.* And signed it *Chris.* I never saw him do it, and I didn't recognise him – but in fact it was Christopher Stamp, former manager of The Who rock group. I've left it there, and have a quiet chuckle every time I look at it.

1 in 'Blue' in 1968

2 at the premiere of 'The Haunted Mansion' in Los Angeles 2003

3 in 'Billy Budd' 1962

4 at 5th Marrakech Film Festival 2005

159

For Terence Stamp, Elena recommends...

Roast Chicken Breast with Sage and Onion Stuffing, Confited Leg, Roast Potatoes and Baby Vegetables

...a favourite with the ladies

Ingredients – serves 4

2 x corn fed chickens
300g Maris Piper potatoes
Mixed baby vegetables of
your choice
150g fresh Japonaise
breadcrumbs
1 onion
50g butter
10 leaves of sage
1 clove garlic
1 bunch thyme
salt and pepper

Method

• Stuffing
• Dice and sweat* onion in butter.
• Add finely chopped sage, salt, pepper.
• Mix with Japonaise breadcrumbs.

Chicken

• Bone chicken so that you have two breasts with wing attached, skin trimmed and two legs.
• For the legs, sprinkle on Maldon sea salt, chopped garlic and thyme, and leave for 8-12 hours.
• Then cook very slowly in simmering duck fat until you can pull the thigh bone out easily.
• Lift half the breast skin and place half the stuffing inside the cavity.
• Season well, and seal in a pan, first flesh side to retain shape. When lightly coloured turn over onto skin, colour a little then place in an oven at 200C Gas Mark 6 for 15 mins.
• In a separate pan heat and place legs skin side down, colour a little then place in oven alongside the breasts for 15 mins.
• Before roasting, peel and cut potatoes and blanch for 10 mins in simmering (not boiling) water. Roast for 15 mins at 200C Gas Mark 6.

Presentation

• To serve, place some baby vegetables in middle of the plate, then place leg and breast on top, and the roasted potatoes around the side. Add some chicken gravy to taste.

5 *at Chelsea Flower Show, London, 2000*

6 *with Dirk Bogarde and Monica Vitti in 'Modesty Blaise' 1966*

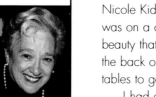

Nicole Kidman

Nicole Kidman came in to L'Etoile, moving very tall and straight as if she was on a catwalk. All that was missing was a book on her head! What a beauty that girl is. She was in a party of six. They had booked a table at the back of the restaurant, which meant that she had to walk past all the tables to get there.

I had a feeling that she had dressed down, in the sense that she was very casual, not at all flamboyant, as if she really didn't want to be noticed. Fat chance of that! The whole place only had eyes for her, as the song goes, and although every one of my waiters is under strict orders: *Don't stare!* I knew my boys were having an inward struggle to keep their eyes off her.

Nicole is close to six feet tall – actually 5ft 10ins – her hair is light and beautiful and she has a skin like porcelain. Perhaps she was born out of her time – she would have been a natural in the thirties. When I greeted her, I was surprised by her unashamed Australian accent, something that for some reason you don't associate with such a slender, statuesque beauty. Well, I don't. Nicole was very animated that day, possibly because she had just been nominated for an Oscar for *The Hours* (and would go on to win it for her performance as Virginia Woolf). I also noticed that she had a good healthy appetite, though where she puts it all heaven alone knows!

When she smiled and took my hand at the end and said some nice things about the restaurant, all I could think of in reply was to follow Stephen Fry's advice with any celebrity: "Keep up the good work!"

1 in 'To Die For' 1995

2 in 'The Interpreter' 2005

3 at the Venice Film Festival 2004

1

Ingredients – serves 4

500g strawberries
6 large egg yolks
90g castor sugar
100g icing sugar
5 tablespoons of champagne
½ teaspoon cornflour
zest of 1 lemon

Method

- Clean berries and halve them. Set aside.
- To make sabayon, put ingredients into a large bowl and whisk until a pale colour.
- Place bowl in a pan of simmering water and whisk to form a foam that will hold its shape in the mix (10-15 mins).
- Just before serving toss berries in icing sugar and 5 tblspns of champagne.
- Divide into 4 small bowls. Spoon sabayon over berries and place under a grill until brown.

Presentation

- Sprinkle with icing sugar and serve.

4 With Ewan McGregor in 'Moulin Rouge'

5 at the New York Premiere of 'Dogville' 2003

6 Studying the script for 'Bewitched' 2005

For Nicole Kidman, Elena recommends...

Gratin of Strawberries, Champagne Sabayon

...perfect anytime

Sting

Sting has been a regular face at all my restaurants, ever since he first walked into Bianchi's with a lovely girl on his arm – who turned out to be Trudie Styler, the actress-turned-producer he would later marry.

He is both amiable and unassuming, and always made reservations in his real name of Gordon Sumner. He was a school teacher in Newcastle, remember, in the days before he found his true calling in the rock world. To meet him, you'd never think his fortune has been estimated at £200 million. Sting also has a great sense of humour, and he found one incident at L'Escargot particularly hilarious.

He arrived with Trudie, by now his wife, and headed for the gents before the meal. Almost on his heels I greeted another regular, Melvyn, *now Lord* Bragg, and watched him head off in the same direction.

Melvyn came out first, wearing a puzzled frown. "Elena," he said. "Let me ask you something: why have you got the police in here today?"

1 with Trudie at Harper's Bazaar relaunch party

2 at home, 1995

3 in the recording studio

I was equally baffled. "Police? What do you mean?"

"Well," Melvyn replied, "I was in the loo and this chap came up and said: 'Hullo! I'm from the police.' He's in there now"

Then Gordon emerged, and still Melvyn didn't recognise him, even though he'd been on the *South Bank Show* a few months earlier. I had to explain: "That's Sting. Don't you know him? His group's the Police."

"Oh God, so it is," said Melvyn – and went over to shake hands, laugh it off, and say hullo to Trudie. On this way back to his own table he passed by me and muttered: "I thought maybe you'd been raided!" I like to think he was joking.

At least Sting took it well "Can you believe Melvyn didn't remember me being on his show? I won't let him forget that in a hurry," he told me.

And I can tell you, he hasn't!

4 Royal Albert Hall in London

5 dressed as Napoleon

Method

- Purée banana in liquidiser with lime juice and 1 tablespoon water.
- Add soaked gelatine, rum and zest of lime.
- Beat hot banana purée into cream cheese. When cool (not cold) fold in cream.
- Whisk egg whites firmly, raining in sugar slowly while whisking.
- Fold into large flan ring with a biscuit base (blend digestive biscuits with butter, press into mould, set in fridge for 1 hour).
- Allow to set for 4 hours in fridge.

Presentation

- Cut into desired portions.
- Finely cut a banana.
- Place slices on top of cheesecake.
- Sprinkle with brown sugar and caramelise.
- Serve either with a raspberry coulis* and seasonal fruits, or chocolate sauce.

Ingredients – serves 6-8 people

500g cream cheese
250g banana
3 egg whites
175g sugar
4 leaves gelatine, soaked 5 mins in cold water
125ml double cream (lightly whipped)
1 shot of rum
juice and zest of 1 lime

Caramelised Banana Cheesecake with Raspberry Coulis and Seasonal Fruits

...so many people's favourite

Emma Thompson

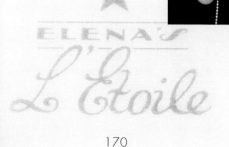

Regal, a luvvie, a little remote? That's the image I suspect a lot of the public has of Emma Thompson, despite the friendly, all-embracing way she comes over whenever I catch her on TV interviews or meet her in the flesh. The truth is a million miles away.

Emma, bless her, is one of the most down-to-earth actresses I've ever met, the sort I would expect to talk about everyday affairs rather than what she wore at last night's film premiere. She would come into L' Etoile with her husband Kenneth Branagh, and their presence attracted all eyes to their table as the perfect celebrity couple.

1 in 'Primary Colors' 1998

2 collecting Best Actress Oscar for 'Howards End in 1992

3 in 'Sense and Sensibility' 1995

4 in 'Look Back in Anger' Lyric Theatre, London, 1989

But I remember her for her laugh and her wicked sense of humour. The Academy Award winning star of *Howard's End* (1992) has taken her place in our 'Oscar' Room, and surely deserves it for putting a sparkle into British films for millions across the world – as well as my restaurants. To show how informal she could be, I remember her sitting on the stairs at L'Escargot next to my husband Aldo, who was in charge of the till, chatting away to him until her table was ready – and sometimes just for a gossip. Aloof? Not our dearest Emma!

Ingredients – serves 4

125g icing sugar
125g soft butter
125g ground walnuts
8 x 4in. puff pastry circles
2 eggs
25g flour
50ml rum
liquid honey

Method

- Beat sugar, walnuts and butter together into a walnut mix(remember to start food mixer slowly and increase the speed).
- Return mixer to 'slow' and add flour.
- Increase speed and add all the eggs one at a time. Stir in rum.
- Place 4 pastry circles on a greased baking tray.
- Score crescent shaped strips in pastry to create 'ball' effect.
- Add a heaped tblspn of walnut mix on top and a little squirt of honey. Leave a ½ in. gap around rim, and paint this with egg yolk.
- Place remaining pastry circles on top and press on to the yolk mix to form a seal.
- Paint top of pithivier with egg yolk.
- Bake in a moderate oven 200C Gas Mark 5-6 for 15-20 min.
- Serve when golden brown with scored pastry on top.

Crème Anglaise*

- Whisk yolks and sugar together in a bowl until white.
- Boil milk and pour onto mix, whisking continuously.
- Return to pan and gently heat, always stirring until mix coats the back of a wooden spoon. Pass through a strainer and serve straight away.

Presentation

- Can also be served cold with a hot pudding.
- To complement the pithivier, whisk ½ teaspoon of walnut oil to Anglaise mix*.

5 with her mother Phyllida Low at London premiere of 'The Winter Guest'

6 in 'Impromptu' 1991

For Emma Thompson, Elena recommends…

Walnut Pithiviers with Crème Anglaise

…a lovely soft centre

1 in 'The Boyfriend' 1971

2&3 in the 1960's

4 with Justin de Villeneuve in 1967

Twiggy

What a sweet girl Twiggy is. She could be anyone's favourite daughter with that pencil-slim model's figure and radiant smile. Twiggy – as in twig, right?

She would come in for lunch with her handsome husband Leigh Lawson – he called her "Twigs" – and always surprised me by her healthy appetite. Somehow, seeing her photographs in all the celebrity magazines, I had assumed she would eat like a little bird. But how wrong can you be! Maybe it was our food – well, I like to think so – but that girl enjoyed our menu as much as anyone. I heard she exercised regularly, with strict self-discipline, so maybe she headed for the gym after lunch!

1

4

SENS UNIQUE

5 Gattinoni fashion show, Milan 2002

6 in New York in 1967

5

Method

Apricot purée

- Take 150g of the apricots, orange juice, 35g sugar and 1 pinch of cinamon. Place apricots in a pan. Pour in orange juice, sugar and cinamon. Boil fruit for 3 min, and allow to cool.
- Liquidise mixture. If too thick, add a little more orange juice to create 300ml apricot purée.

Mousse

- Place milk in a saucepan with 1 tblspn sugar and bring to the boil.
- Whisk yolks and 50g sugar together until white or pale.
- Pour the milk on to yolk mix, and mix together, then return to the pan and cook very slowly for 3-4 mins or until you can make a line on the back of a wooden spoon with your finger.
- Add the pre-soaked gelatine, squeeze first, mix in then pass through a strainer.
- Add apricot purée, mix well and chill until just on melting point.
- Whip cream to soft peaks, and fold into mix.
- Stiffly whip whites, raining in 25g of sugar after 2 mins.
- Fold into milk.
- Wipe inside of some individual moulds with a non-flavoured oil. Put mix into moulds and allow to set.
- To turn out, dip moulds in very hot water for 4 secs. Ease mousse away from sides to release the vacuum, and turn out.

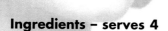

Ingredients – serves 4

Purée ingredients
250g dried apricot halves
125ml orange juice
35g castor sugar
pinch cinamon
Mousse ingredients
300ml apricot purée
125ml double cream
4 leaves gelatine (soaked in cold water for 5 mins).
3 egg yolks
3 egg whites
75g castor sugar
250 ml milk
100g raspberries
1 bunch fresh mint

6

Presentation

- Take remainder of apricot halves and cut into cubes and slices.
- Fan slices on top of each mousse and place cubes around the plate.
- Add a few raspberries cut in halves and place and crush remainder to make a jus.
- Drizzle a little apricot purée and the raspberry jus around the plate.
- Finish with a few leaves of fresh mint.

Apricot Bavarois

...classically beautiful

1 in 'Charlie Chan and the Curse of the Dragon Queen' 1981

2 admitted to the French Fine Art Academy, Paris, 1989

3 receiving his Oscar for Best Supporting Actor in 'Spartacus' from Eve Marie Saint in 1961

Peter Ustinov

2

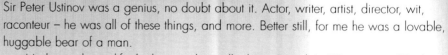

3

Sir Peter Ustinov was a genius, no doubt about it. Actor, writer, artist, director, wit, raconteur – he was all of these things, and more. Better still, for me he was a lovable, huggable bear of a man.

My heart always lifted whenever he walked into Bianchi's, L'Escargot or L'Etoile – he frequented all three, and became as close to being a friend of the family as any of the celebrities I see daily. He would sit on the stairs at L'Escargot, easing his large bulk

on to the top step, and chat away to Aldo at the till, laughing and joking with him until it was time to eat. One day he suddenly produced a sheet of paper, and sat there scrawling away as he talked. When he got up, he presented my husband with the result – which we treasure to this day. It was a cartoon of himself, with the words: *To Aldo, with friendship*. The day Peter passed away I felt a personal sadness, because we all knew the world had lost someone who was genuinely irreplaceable.

For Peter Ustinov, Elena recommends...

Tart Tatin with Calvados Crème Fraiche

...so many fans around the world

Ingredients – serves 4

8 Braeburn or Granny Smiths
apples
2 x 25cm puff pastry circles,
4mm thick
180g castor sugar
90g butter
good pinch of cinnamon

Method

- Peel and core apples and cut into quarters.
- Pre-heat oven to 200C Gas Mark 6.
- Slice butter finely and place on bottom of a non stick saucepan Sprinkle with sugar and cinnamon.
- Press apple quarters into butter, arranging in a circle.
- Place saucepan on a medium gas ring, cook for 10-12 mins, occasionally rolling pan and checking if caramel is forming.
- Remove from heat. Lay pastry over the top and tuck the edges down side of pan with a spatula.
- Place in oven and cook at 180C Gas Mark 4 for 12-15 mins, or until pastry is golden brown.
- Remove and cool for 10 mins.
- Then turn out very carefully, protecting pastry base.

Presentation

- Serve with crème fraiche, calvados crème fraiche,* clotted cream or vanilla ice cream.

4 in 'Appointment with Death' 1988

5 in Quo Vadis 1951

6 Self Portrait for Elena's husband Aldo, drawn on the stairs at L'Escargot

5

Per Aldo
Con Amicizia

6

Samantha Morton

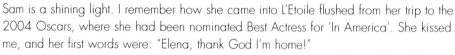

Sam is a shining light. I remember how she came into L'Etoile flushed from her trip to the 2004 Oscars, where she had been nominated Best Actress for 'In America'. She kissed me, and her first words were: "Elena, thank God I'm home!"

Well, that wasn't quite the remark I expected from someone who had been feted from the moment she set foot in tinsel town, and given the VIP treatment, the full works, from dawn till dusk. "Come on, Sam," I said. "You can't mean that. You must have had a wonderful time."

"Of course I did," she responded. "They spoiled me rotten. But I honestly can't bear all that Hollywood razzmatazz. It's just not me. I simply want to be home with my little

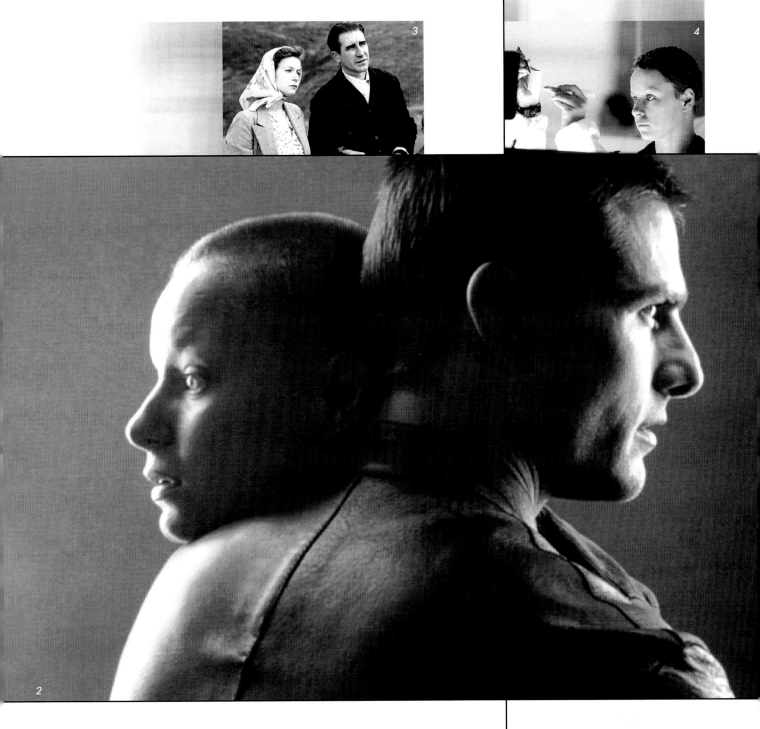

girl." The little girl being her daughter Esme, then aged 4 and the apple of her mother's eye.

"I understand, my dear," I told her. "I'm just the same."

She's gloriously down to earth, that girl. Not an inch of side on her, and I'd go so far as to say that she's even a little shy under the public microscope. I think Sam's going to be a great star – just watch her. As for *not* getting the Oscar, she wasn't upset at all. Or if she was, she didn't show it.

But then I've always said: those actors put on the best performance of their lives when they lose! Just watch them smile and applaud as the winner walks up to make the big thank you speech – and you wonder what they're *really* thinking inside.

1 in 'Sweet and Lowdown' 1999

2 with Tom Cruise in 'Minority Report' 2002

3 with John Lynch in 'Lassie' 2005

4 in 'Code 46' 2004

ELENA'S
L'Étoile

5 *with Rupert Graves in 'Dreaming of Joseph Lees' 1999*

6 *with Paddy Considine in 'In America' 2002*

Ingredients – serves 4

For syrup
375g castor sugar
325ml water
1 lemon sliced
35g liquid glucose

For Sorbet
250g raspberries
juice of ½ lemon
150ml sorbet syrup*

Method

- To form the syrup, boil the water, castor sugar, sliced lemon and glucose in saucepan for 2 mins to reduce to one third and strain.

- Pour warm syrup and lemon juice at 70C on to raspberries and leave to mascarate for 45 mins.
- Blend in a liquidiser and pass through a fine sieve.
- Place in ice-cream machine and churn until semi-firm, then place in freezer until required.

For Samantha Morton, Elena recommends...

Raspberry Sorbet

...always cool and fresh

Annie Lennox

Annie Lennox had booked a table for two in L'Etoile, and she walked in with another woman I recognised immediately: Anita Roddick, founder and driving force behind the amazing Body Shop chain. I have no idea how these two ladies got together, but they seemed to be close friends for a lively luncheon.

At the end, we got chatting, and Annie said something that made my day – and my week! She looked at me and declared: "Elena, what wonderful skin you've got. It belongs to a woman half your age, and you've got the energy to go with it." And Anita chimed in: "I tell you what, Elena. If you tell me your secret, I'll bottle it and make a fortune!" She had made one fortune already, so I didn't feel too guilty about telling her what I tell everyone: "It's hard work, pure and simple. That's what keeps me young!" And it's true

1 at premiere of 'The Chronicles of Narnia – The Lion The Witch and the Wardrobe' London, 2005

2 at Nelson Mandela concert Cape Town, 2003

3 at World Health Organisation Conference, London 2006

4 with Dave Stewart at Eurythmics –'Ultimate Collection' party 2005

187

5 with Eurythmics partner Dave Stewart at Brit Awards, London 1984

6 at Nelson Mandela Foundation concert South Africa 2005

Method

- Pour water and 50g sugar into a saucepan and bring to boil.
- Place thermometer into pan.
- Whisk yolks in a separate heat-proof bowl with a hand held electric whisk until thick and pale.
- Heat to 118C soft ball stage, take off heat and with electric whisk running on full speed trickle the syrup on to the yolk mix.
- Continue until all syrup is incorporated. Whisk for a further 2 mins and set aside.
- Make mango puree by taking 1 kilo of very ripe mango. Peel and chop flesh. Place in liquidiser or food processor with passion fruit juice, and blend. If too thick to blend fully, add a little orange juice.
- Whisk double cream to soft peaks and fold into mix.
- Whisk egg whites and allow to gain air for 3-4 mins before slowly raining in the sugar.
- Whisk stiffly and fold into the mix.
- Cut passion fruit in half, scoop out pulp, pass through a sieve into a bowl pressing hard. Retain juice, discard pips and skin.
- Add lime juice, zest and mango purée.
- Mix yolk mixture in a large bowl with mango purée, passion fruit juice, lime juice and zest together.
- Place in a terrine mould lined with cling film or use individual lightly oiled moulds. Freeze the mix.

Ingredients – serves 6

150ml double cream
1kg very ripe mango
zest and juice of 2 limes
6 passion fruits
5 egg yolks
2 egg whites
100ml water
150g castor sugar

Presentation

- To demould terrine, leave at room temperature for 5-10 mins, then turn out and slice for individual moulds.
- Dip into very hot water 2-3 secs, then turn out straight on to serving plate.
- Serve with raspberry coulis* and exotic fruits.

Mango, Passion Fruit & Lime Iced Parfait

...the energy fruit

Peter O'Toole

Peter O'Toole came wandering off the street into L'Etoile one lunchtime, and took me completely by surprise. He asked if I had a table free. I hadn't seen him in ten years, but of course I recognised him immediately. "Why, Mr O'Toole, how wonderful to see you again!" I exclaimed. He bent his gaze on me. "Have we met?" he inquired. "Of course," I retorted. "From the days of L'Escargot and Bianchi's, don't you remember?" He looked closer. "Good Lord," he said. "Why, it's Elena!"

Then he bent lower, and said almost furtively: "Listen, Elena, I need a table for six. I've got some very important people coming today. Can you help me out?" We were close to full, but I found him a table in a corner, just as five Indian gentlemen walked in. Throughout the lunch the six of them sat huddled together deep in conversation, all very intense, and at the end they insisted on being photographed against one of the walls with all our pictures on it. Then Peter waved me in to join them for a photo. "We're discussing a film, it's called *Venus*," he confided, on the way out. "We need a scene in a restaurant like this. Could we use your pictures from the walls?"

This put me in a quandary, because I would never let my pictures out. They're part of the atmosphere, and far too precious. I said: "I'm sorry, I can't. But if you want to send someone round to my house, I've got copies there that you can photograph." Sure enough, someone did come round a few days later to my house in Islington with a camera, and spent an hour photographing the pictures I kept in a drawer.

That was the last I heard of it. In fact, I'd forgotten all about it until this year – when I saw that the film *Venus* was in line for a possible Academy Award in 2007, with the Walt Disney company putting their weight behind Peter O'Toole for the best actor Oscar! He's 74 now, and like Richard Burton had been nominated seven times without ever winning. I'd had no idea what the film was about, but now I learned that he plays an ageing thespian who becomes besotted with a young girl, played by a newcomer named Jodie Whittaker. Win or lose, I'd keep my fingers crossed for him. I never could understand why he didn't win an Oscar for *Lawrence of Arabia*. As for the restaurant, he came in again four times in that one week, either with a business friend or a lady. Since then, I haven't seen him once!

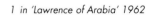

1 in 'Lawrence of Arabia' 1962

2 with Peter Sellers in 'What's New Pussycat' 1965

3 in 'My Favourite Year' 1982

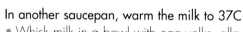

4 in 'The Last Emperor 1987

5 at The Coach and Horses pub in Soho 1989

Ingredients – serves 4

225g dark chocolate
200g white chocolate
80g unsalted butter
100g castor sugar
150ml double cream
40g cocoa powder
4 egg yolks
3 gellatine
1 pod vanilla
1 bay leaf
1 bunch mint
1 star anis
100ml milk
550ml cold water

Sponge Mix
100g plain flour
100g corn flour
250g castor sugar
8 egg yolks
8 egg whites
zest of 1 lemon
4 sponge ring moulds

Method
Sponge mix

- Place castor sugar, lemon zest and 8 egg yolks in a medium sizes bowl.
- Whisk until mix forms ribbon like texture.
- In a separate bowl whisk 8 egg whites until volume is trebled
- Very slowly, fold in all the plain flour and half the corn flour creating a light form and texture.
- Pour the egg white mix into a pastry tray covered with grease proof paper, well greased with butter on all sides.
- Bake in oven at 200C Gas Mark 6 for 8 mins until golden colour.
- Allow to cool before cutting into rings using the sponge ring moulds.

Method
Chocolate mix

- Place broken white chocolate in one bowl and broken dark chocolate in another bowl, each with half the butter.
- Place each bowl over a saucepan of barely simmering water.
- Ensure that the bowls do not touch the water and that heat is at its lowest.
- Allow both chocolates to melt for 6 mins.
- Remove bowls from heat, stir well and allow to cool for 3 mins.
- Place 450ml of cold water in a saucepan.
- Add 200g castor sugar, the vanilla pod (cut in half with seeds removed), the star anis and bay leaf.
- Bring water mix to the boil and reduce by ½ until a thick syrup forms.
- Meanwhile, whisk the cocoa powder in another saucepan with 60ml of cold water.
- Place on a high heat and mix with half the syrup.
- Allow to cool and mix into the bowl of dark chocolate.

In another saucepan, warm the milk to 37C

- Whisk milk in a bowl with egg yolks, allow to cool and place in the bowl of white chocolate.
- Take remainder of the flavoured syrup, heat in a saucepan till hot and add to milk and egg yolk mix. Allow to cook for 4 mins, then cool.
- Soak the gelatine leaves in cold water for 10 mins to completely dissolve.
- Whisk double cream until thick and divide, half in each of the dark and white chocolate bowls, stir in very slowly until full integrated.

For Peter O'Toole, Elena recommends...

Chocolate Torte

...there's no harm in a little hedonism

Presentation

- Simply remove the double chocolate torte from the moulds
- Add a thin coating of the remaining dark chocolate as a finishing touch
- Place on dessert plate and drizzle with Crème Anglaise sauce*
- Garnish with a leaf of mint and a few fresh raspberries around the plate

Line up the 4 moulds

- Begin by placing the 5cm round sponge shapes at the bottom as a base.
- Half fill each mould by spooning in the dark chocolate mix – but leave about 10% for the finishing touch.
- Place on a tray and chill in the refrigerator for a minimum 4 hours to set.
- Remove and add the white chocolate mix to fill the moulds and return to the refrigerator for a further 4 hours.

193

Joanne Whalley Kilmer

One of my regulars Jane Robinson, who designed clothes for films, dropped in to announce: "Elena, Joanne Whalley has to meet the director of *Scandal* to talk about Christine Keeler. They're casting it now. They're meeting here for lunch." The year was 1988, the director was Michael Caton-Jones, and I'd never met either of them before.

Jane said: "I've got some clothes with me. She really wants the part. What I've got in mind is that Joanne should meet him looking just like Keeler, and dressed for the role! Can you help by giving her somewhere to change? It's got to be a big surprise."

I said: "Don't worry. I'll take her upstairs to a private room." That's when Joanne came in wearing jeans and a sweater, looking quite ordinary really, and I led her through to a room upstairs.

1 in 'Kill Me Again' 1989

2 with Bridget Fonda in 'Scandal' 1989

1 2

The director duly arrived, and I took him to his table. Then I collected Joanne. I couldn't believe the transformation!" She came down the stairs like a tigress, wearing the sexy Keeler outfit that everyone knows from the newspapers. She looked stunning. I escorted her over to the table and announced formally: "Mr Caton-Jones – meet Christine Keeler!"

His jaw dropped almost to the table. Joanne sat down, they talked animatedly for the whole meal – and by the end of it she had the job. Afterwards Joanne said to me: "You must come to the premiere." And I did. Joanne swept in to the foyer among all the lights and flashing cameras, and I caught her eye. She dropped me a big wink, that said it all."

ELENA'S

L'Etoile

3 in 'Trial by Jury' 1994

4 in 'Navy S E A L S' 1990

5 with John Hurt in 'Scandal' 1989

3

Ingredients – serves 6-8

500mm double cream
½ pt milk
7 large egg yolks
80g sugar
1 large vanilla pod

Method

- Slice vanilla pod in half length-ways, and scrape out the seeds. Place in a bowl with egg yolks.
- Add sugar and beat into yolks.
- Add milk and cream.
- Pass mixture through a sieve.
- Drop remaining vanilla bean into mixture and leave for 2 hrs.
- Pre-heat oven to 140C Gas Mark 1.
- Pour mixture into ramekin. Put into a water bath and place in oven for 40-50 mins until mixture is set.
- Allow to cool and then chill until required.

Presentation

- Sprinkle demerara evenly over the brulée.
- Tip off excess sugar.
- Clean sides of ramekin, then caramelise top with a blow torch.
- Serve straight away.

4

5

For Joanne Whalley Kilmer, Elena recommends...

Crème Brûlée

...a 'scandalous' dessert

*Definitions, Stocks, Sauces, Garnishes

Definitions

'Sweating'
To 'sweat' place ingredients in a fry pan on a very low heat for 2-3 mins to release flavour using either butter or olive oil.

'Al dente'
Cooking vegetables only until they remain slightly crunchy.

'Con – Casse' – tomatoes
Blanch in boiling water for a few seconds then remove skin and dice or shape as preferred.

'Demi – glass'
Add substance to a sauce or liquid.

Stocks, sauces, garnishes

Salt Cod (Croquettes of Salt Cod, Langoustine and Crab)
* Leave for eight hours in this mix, turning occasionally.
1kg cod
35g rock salt
15g sugar
1 star anise
juice of 3 lemons
1 small pinch of saffron
1 measure of Pernod

Sweetcorn Butter (Croquettes of Salt Cod, Langoustine and Crab)
* Blend the following together
225ml white wine
225ml langoustine stock
225ml Vermouth
1 shallot finely chopped
1 small bunch of thyme
qtr of a bay leaf
2 corn on the cobs
225g unsalted butter

Rouille (Croquettes of Salt Cod, Langoustine and Crab)
* Blend the following together.
1 red pepper skinned
2 cloves of garlic
1 boiled egg grated or sieved
250 ml olive oil
250 ml vegetable oil
3 egg yolks
1 tablespoon Dijon mustard
pinch of cayenne

Lamb stock (Confit of Welsh Lamb)
* Roast lamb bones at 200C Gas Mark 6 for 20 mins.
* Add roughly chopped root vegetables – brown well.
* Into colander from oven to remove fat.
* Deglaze bottom of pan using half bottle red wine to lift caramelised pieces.
* Pour into saucepan to cover bones.
* Add bouquet garni and cold water.
* Simmer 3 hours.

Caper sauce (Confit of Welsh Lamb)
* Sweat 1 finely sliced shallot and 1 clove garlic.
* Add 250ml white wine, 250ml chicken stock 50ml caper vinegar.
* Heat to reduce by two thirds. Add 500ml double cream and reduce by a third.
* Add 2 tblsp of fine capers and 1 tblsp fine chopped flat parsley.

Rosemary Jus (Saddle of Lamb)
* Reduce 1 cup of red wine and 1 cup brown stock* to ¼.
* Demi-glass the sauce with fresh Rosemary to add substance.
* Add ½ cup Madeira to flavour.

Bechamel Sauce – (Salmon and Leek Fishcake)
100g flour
100ml milk
knob of unsalted butter
pinch nutmeg
salt and pepper
Method
* Melt butter in pan.
* When bubbling, but before turning brown, add flour through wire sieve.
* Stir gently with a wooden spoon into a thick creamy substance.
* Add *hot* milk, stir vigorously.
* Season with salt, pepper and a little nutmeg.
* Add salmon juice retained from cooking.
* Sauce should be thick.

Mustard Sauce (Veal Kidneys)
1 shallot
½ cup white wine
⅓ cup chicken stock*
2 tbsp wholegrain mustard
Method
* Cut 1 shallot very small and sweat* until colourless.
* Add ½ cup white wine and ⅓ cup chicken stock*.
* Season with salt and pepper.
* Reduce the sauce by ¾.
* Demi-glass the sauce with 100ml double cream and add 2 tbsps of wholegrain mustard.

Green Chive Sauce (Fillet of Poached Cod)
1 sliced Spanish onion
½ lemon
1 star anis
½ bunch thyme
½ cup white wine
1 bunch chives
½ cup chicken stock
200ml double cream
Method
* Sweat onion in butter or olive oil.
* Add chicken stock, wine ,lemon, thyme and star anis.
* Reduce by three quarters.
* Add cream and chives and season.
* Leave until 'sticky'.

Hollandaise sauce
(Feuillete Asparagus)
3 egg yolks
200ml tarragon white wine vinegar
100g unsalted butter
salt and pepper
Method
- Mix 200ml tarragon white wine vinegar with 3 egg yolks, whisking in a bowl until stiff.
- Melt 100g butter in a small non stick saucepan.
- Pour and stir butter slowly into the egg yolk mix to create the classic hollandaise sauce.
- Season with salt and pepper.

Cep Sauce – serves 4
(Ribeye Steak/Roast Sea Bass)
1 Spanish onion
1 cup white wine
250ml chicken stock
100g dried cep mushrooms (soaked)
handful fresh cep mushrooms
1 bouquet garni
250ml double cream
150ml Vermouth
salt and black pepper
Method
- Sweat* finely chopped onion until colourless.
- Add dried Cep mushrooms.
- Add white wine, chicken stock, bouquet garni and Vermouth.
- Reduce by ½.
- Season with salt and black pepper.
- Add cream and blend in a liquidiser until creamy. Cook for further 10 mins
- Pass through a fine sieve.
- Sautee and sprinkle a few fresh ceps on the sauce.

Mushy Peas – serves 4
(Salmon and Leek Fishcake)
400g frozen peas
1 bunch fresh mint
½ lemon
salt and pepper
1 tblspn olive oil
Method
- Thaw peas in water for 10 mins.
- Place in a bowl, add mint, lemon, olive oil and season.
- Blend for approx 1 minute and serve.

Elena's Chips – serves 4 (Salmon and Leek Fishcake/Ribeye Steak)
- Take 4 large Maris Piper potatoes.
- Peel and cut into preferred size and shape.
- Shallow fry in hot sunflower oil till crisp.
- Add Maldon Sea Salt to taste.

Sauce Bercy (Seared Scallops)
1 shallot
½ cup white wine
½ cup fish stock
200ml double cream
½ bunch thyme
½ lemon
1 stanis
Method
- Sweat shallot for 2-3 mins.
- Add all other ingredients and reduce to a quarter.
- Add double cream creating a 'thick' texture.

Fish Sauce (Poached Halibut)
200ml double cream
1 diced Spanish onion
½ cup white wine
½ cup fish stock
salt and pepper
Method
- Slice the Spanish onion, sweat* in a non stick saucepan until there is no colour.
- Add the ½ cup white wine and ½ cup fish stock.
- Raise heat and reduce the sauce to ¼ of volume.
- 200ml double cream to demi-glass (add substance) and pepper, and check the seasoning.

Fish Stock – serves 4
- 600g fish bones (lemon sole or langoustine as preferred).
- Place in medium saucepan, add bouquet garni and cover with water.
- Bring to boil and simmer for 30 mins.
- Leave to cool.

Croutons – 100g (Fish Soup)
3 medium slices of white bread
2 cloves garlic
½ bunch thyme
Method
- Cut bread in to small cubes (2cm).
- Heat olive oil in a shallow pan to medium temp.
- Add cubes of bread.
- Add garlic cloves and thyme.
- Pass through a conical strainer.
- Leave to cool.

Plain Mayonnaise
(Lobster Salad)
3 egg yolks
1 whole egg
1 tblspn Dijon mustard
100ml extra virgin olive oil
Method
- Blend three egg yolks and 1 whole egg in a food mixer.
- Add 1 tblspn French Dijon mustard.
- Slowly pour 100ml extra virgin olive oil to emulsify the eggs.
- Continue blending until mix is thorough and stiff.

Garlic Mayonnaise (Fish Soup)
2 cloves garlic
5 egg yolks
2 whole eggs
500ml oil (olive or vegetable)
Method
- Place eggs in food mixer and churn slowly for 2 mins.
- Add finely chopped garlic.
- Gradually add oil to mixture while increasing churn speed.
- Season to taste and serve.

Vinaigrette (Rare Grilled Tuna)
100ml balsamic vinager
400ml vegetable oil
100g Dijon French mustard
- Mix all ingredients in a food processor until thick.

Greek yoghurt sauce
(Rare Grilled Tuna)
600ml Greek yoghurt
3 leaves fresh mint

continued over

1 tspn Chinese fish sauce (Squid brand)
salt and pepper

- Mix all ingredients in a small bowl and stir to create a smooth creamy sauce.

Brown Sauce

100ml red wine
1 bouquet garni
1 miracroix (containing 1 of each of carrot, onion, thyme, garlic clove, leek)
100g beef trimmings
250ml water

Method

- Drizzle oil in a large saucepan.
- Place on medium heat.
- Add miracroix and bouquet garni.
- Cover with water and add red wine.
- Reduce to one third.

Madeira Gravy (Beef Wellington)

Add 200ml Madeira, 200ml Port, 200ml red wine.

Brown Gravy (Calves Liver)

- Add 200ml Port and 3 shallots, sliced and fried.

Lemon and Chive Butter (Potato Pancake with Wild Smoked Salmon)

1 Spanish onion
½ lemon
100ml white wine
100ml chicken stock*
100g butter
1 bouquet garni
1 bunch chives
salt and pepper

Method

- Sweat onion in saucepan for 2 mins.
- Add white wine, chicken stock, bouquet garni and ½ lemon (retaining the zest).
- Reduce to a quarter.
- Slice butter and add to mix with wooden spoon.
- Stir until thick adding chopped chives
- Season to taste.
- Finish with lemon zest.

Choucroute (Sauerkraut)-serves 4 (Roast Salmon Potato Crust)

1 large carrot

1 white cabbage
100ml white wine vinegar
100ml white wine
1 bouquet garni
4 rashers streaky bacon
50g wrapped juniper berries

Method

- Slice cabbage very finely using a Japonaise Mandolin.
- Cut bacon into pieces and place in a large saucepan with bouquet garni for 5-10mins on a high heat.
- Add white wine, vinegar and juniper.
- Add white cabbage.
- Cook on high heat for a further 5-10 mins.
- Then simmer with lid on for 30 mins until cabbage assumes a soft texture.
- Cool and place in refrigerator.

Chicken Stock serves 4

1 miracroix (carrot, onion, leek, celery)
1 bouquet garni
600g chicken bones
200ml water

Method

- Place chicken bones in large saucepan.
- Add miracroix and bouquet garni.
- Cover with water.
- Bring to boil and simmer with lid on for 1 hr 20mins.

Pommes Fondant – serves 4 (Roast Guinea Fowl)

4 large Maris Piper baked potatoes
½ bunch thyme
3 cloves garlic
250ml chicken stock
100g unsalted butter

Method

- Place knob butter in a large saucepan.
- Add garlic and thyme.
- Cut potatos, remove ends and peel into 3 inch cylinder shapes.
- Add the 4 cut potatoes to the saucepan.
- Cook on a high heat until golden brown.
- Add chicken stock to immerse one third of the potatoes.
- Place lid on saucepan to steam for 30-45 minutes on a low heat.
- Remove lid. Increase to high heat to remove excess stock.

Raspberry Coulis (Caramelised Banana Cheesecake)

250g raspberries
50g castor sugar
Juice from ½ lemon

Method

- Blend ingredients and pass through a sieve.
- If too thick add a little water.
- Add more sugar to sweeten further to taste.

Calvados Crème Fraiche – serves 4 (Tart Tatin)

200ml double cream
100g castor sugar
100ml white wine
2 tblspns banana essence
100ml Calvados

Method

- Place sugar, wine, banana essence and Calvados in small saucepan.
- Reduce to syrup and cool.
- Whip cream to medium texture.
- Fold syrup into cream and refrigerate.

Crème Anglaise – serves 4 (Walnut Pithiviers)

6 egg yolks
125g castor sugar
500ml milk
1 vanilla pod, split
½ tspn walnut oil

Method

- Whisk yolks and sugar together in a bowl until white.
- Boil milk and pour onto mix, whisking continuously.
- Return to pan and gently heat, always stirring until mix coats the back of a wooden spoon. Pass through a strainer and serve straight away.
- Can also be served cold with a hot pudding.
- To complement the pithiviers, whisk ½ teaspoon of walnut oil to Anglaise mix.

Recipe Notes

Recipe Notes

About the Walnut team

William Hall is internationally known as Michael Caine's official biographer and is currently promoting the latest edition – *70 Not Out*. Another dozen other best-selling biographies include James Dean, Norman Wisdom and Frankie Howerd. A distinguished film critic and past President of the elite Critics' Circle he was both film editor of the London Evening News and a frequent contributor to the LA Times. He has interviewed all the great screen legends from Charlie Chaplin to John Wayne, Marlon Brando and Elizabeth Taylor, and today's stars like Tom Cruise, Halle Berry and Pierce Brosnan. A world exclusive was an hour with Elvis Presley. William Hall is currently writing his own biography *Hall of Fame*.

Mike Maloney OBE was, until recently, Chief Photographer at Trinity Mirror newspapers. Over a thirty year career with Mirror Group he has won 100 photo-journalism awards, more than any of his peers. Mike was awarded the OBE in the 2005 New Year honours list. From royalty to showbiz; sport to politics; hard news to features – Mike not only photographed stars like Grace Kelly, Frank Sinatra, Madonna, Sir Paul McCartney and Kylie, he even became known as 'the Queen Mum's favourite press photographer.' Mike is also an entertaining lecturer, columnist and speaker on photography.

Chris Wright MCIPR is an accomplished PR and marketing consultant who has worked in lifestyle markets including hotels, restaurants, fashion, casinos and sport, as well as retailing, industry and technology. As MD of WSM Wordsworth Limited Chris was retained by The Restaurant Partnership plc when it teamed Elena with the equally legendary L'Etoile. It was while working for Elena's L'Etoile on the centenary celebrations for the restaurant that the Walnut team first co-operated together. They created the now famous 'Centenary Private Room' at the restaurant which is dedicated to British Oscar Winners and raises much gold each year for The Actors Charitable Trust home, Denville Hall.

Acknowledgements

All celebrity archive pictures supplied by
Rex Features www.rexfeatures.com
Special thanks to: Glen Marks, Stephen Atkinson, The Everett Collection
and SIPA.

Film and other stills from The Everett Collection
Columbia Pictures, Miramax Films, Warner Bros, MGM, 20th Century Fox,
MCA/Universal, Buena Vista Pictures, Sony Pictures, PBS, Touchstone,
Hemdale, Savoy Pictures, Paramount Pictures, United Artists, Roadside
Attractions, REN, Atlantic, First Look, Focus, Orion, Cinecom Pictures, Rank.

Photographers and Sources
Nils Jorgensen, Richard Young, Ken McKay, Alistair Linford, Geoff Wilkinson,
Brian Rasic, ML Antonelli, News International, Snap.

Biography section photographers
Alan Raymond, Oscar Lasa Photography, Trevor Humphries.

Notable friends and supporters
Corus Hotels plc
The Restaurant Partnership plc
Roy Ackerman CBE
Nick Scade MBE
Paul Breach
Pascal and Kim Schnyder (Casa Pascal, Pattaya, Thailand)